ELEVATE

How to lift the quality of thinking in your team's board papers without rewriting them yourself

Davina Stanley

Disclaimer

You provide a really clear and concise roadmap to quality board presentations and the methodologies needed to get the best team results.

Wayne Lewis, Board Chair, Ballarat Hospital

Before I read Elevate, *preparing board papers was a chore. Davina Stanley has opened my eyes to the great opportunity that exists as a senior leader to not only build the capability of my team, but also efficiently extract enormous value from the board reporting process. I highly commend this focused and practical guide and suggest it should be the standard approach adopted by organisations everywhere.*

Daniel Musson, Chief Experience Officer, Australian Meat Industry Superannuation Fund

Elevate *is an engaging, punchy and pragmatic book that will help you communicate better. It reminds us all to get to the very heart of the matter, and to think of communication as a valued corporate competence and source of competitive advantage. Implementing the invaluable lessons within the book will encourage more insightful thinking and inevitably deliver real commercial value to your organisation.*

Adam Bennett, former CEO, NSW Land Registry Services

This guide is so effective for teaching and embedding more powerful communication within a team. Elevate *is enjoyable and easy to read with relatable content and stories of the all too familiar and painful paper review cycles we find ourselves in. I love Davina's practical advice for how to break unproductive patterns to save time and to empower leaders and contributors.*

Her detailed workshop schedule and metrics to track tangible improvement are so valuable, her book is now required reading in my team!

Jasmine Parer, Service Design Lead, HSBC

Contents

Acknowledgements

Many people have helped me write this book – not least the many clients who have let me help with their communication.

Some, however, deserve to be called out as they have been closely involved with this project and its companion book, *Engage*.

My 'brains trust'. Brendon Jones, Brian Edler, Brooke El Azzi, Clement Armstrong, Mike Sherman, Phil Leacock and Ravi David have been long-time collaborators who have stretched my thinking. Jasmine Parer, Louise Cornelis and Wayne Lewis were also generous with their time and suggestions.

My inspirations. I stand on big shoulders, having begun my career as a communication specialist at McKinsey in Hong Kong, and having access to the ideas of the Firm's greatest communicators. Having my Pyramid Principle training evaluated by Barbara Minto of Pyramid Principle fame also inspired me to push myself harder to master structured communication techniques.

I also very much appreciate smart questions from colleagues such as James Deighton. James years ago presciently asked me questions like, 'But ... how do we get the team to actually do this?' These led me to think about implementing structured thinking from a leadership standpoint, which in turn led to this book.

My colleagues, past and present. Your enthusiasm and challenge over the years has been invaluable. Sheena, Fatima and Maria, my personal team, you have been indispensable.

My family. My toughest and most valuable critics.

Introduction

It's 9 pm and you're turning to your laptop to review the pre-reading your team has prepared for the coming senior leadership meeting.

You sigh. You'd much prefer to be watching Netflix, tucking into a book or having an early night. But having been swamped with meetings for the past week, you have again left this review to the last minute. You flicked through it days ago but could tell it wasn't ready – and a lot of time would be needed to get it there.

The team has a great plan, but your quick look told you their draft will not cut it.

You are frustrated that you can't quickly find the key messages that will land with your leadership team. The framing is off. The nuggets are buried. Long lists of relevant facts are scattered throughout without being woven into the central narrative.

Without the paper providing high-quality insights that are easily digested, you will spend the leadership meeting answering basic questions rather than discussing the issues.

You will most likely leave with more questions than answers and without the decision you need. And you haven't had a block of focus time to deal with it.

Darn. You must settle in for a long night. Yet again, you must dig in to find the nuggets you know are there and frame them so they resonate with the leadership team.

This is a delicate dance as you aim to keep as much of your team's work as possible so you don't crush them, while lifting the messaging.

You turn in at midnight wondering whether you have done your team's ideas justice and whether the paper will get the decision you need or just more questions.

Does this sound familiar?

Many leaders tell me they assume it is their job to rework hundreds of pages of their team's work each weekend. It is 'normal' to rework their team's papers out of hours. It comes with the territory.

But ... does it need to?

I don't think so.

I've seen many leaders turn this around and look forward to helping you do the same.

Wouldn't it be amazing if you and your teams consistently got better, faster decisions from papers and presentations that are (mostly!) written and reviewed within working hours?

Imagine having time to think, and getting much of your nights and weekends back.

This book helps you do that. I first help you lay strong foundations, and then lift yourself out of the detail before elevating your team's capabilities. Here's a preview.

▲ Lay strong foundations

I begin by introducing a new way to think about the foundations for papers and presentations. Instead of focusing on the words and images you see in the document, I explore the underbelly. How do you set your team up to clarify the thinking that underpins great papers and presentations?

Chapter 1. Think differently about your communication: In this chapter, I help you to focus on what matters, discover where the opportunities are, set targets and see what others have achieved. By the end, you will be thinking more about decisions and less about documents.

Chapter 2. Iterate fast and early: I introduce a new way of collaborating to get the best from you and each of your team. This means inserting yourself into the process both earlier and less.

▲ Lift out of the detail

Now it's time to see how my Elevate framework sets you all up to succeed. I help you guide your team as they clarify and convey insights that resonate with decision-makers in four steps.

Chapter 3. *Ready your team.* I help you leverage your insight and experience to cut wasted effort. I help you set the team up to think strategically about the outcome this communication will deliver, and potentially also what the high-level narrative structure might look like.

Chapter 4. Iterate the message. This is the engine for your approach. The vast bulk of the value for you and the team lies in 'nailing' a highly-structured one-page

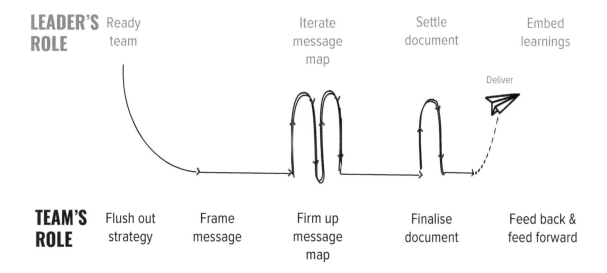

message map before preparing any kind of document. I illustrate how to lean on thinking structures to find holes in the messaging and differentiate strong from weak while working at pace.

Chapter 5. Settle the document. Now the messaging is clear, these documents come together quickly. I explain how to check whether the team has maintained the integrity of the messaging from the one-page message map into the paper or presentation, regardless of whether you are working free-form or confined by a corporate template.

Chapter 6. Embed the learning. This is an essential, often overlooked, investment in all of your nights and weekends. A quick conversation can help you all learn what worked, what didn't and why so you can take it forward.

▲ Elevate your team

After lifting yourself out of the details, it's time to help you help your team.

Chapter 7. Engage your team. Now you see how to iterate fast and early around message maps, it is time to prepare your team to do likewise. First, you need to get them onboard so they understand the value it brings to them, to the organisation and to you.

Chapter 8. Lift your team's skills. Now it is time to help them define their desired outcome, understand their audience, synthesise and structure their message and visualise that message effectively in paper or presentation format.

Chapter 9. Flourish into the long term. How often do new initiatives run out of steam after the initial enthusiasm wears off? For marginally little effort, you will see the compounding effect of operationalising the approach. I help you embed the behaviours, habits and expectations.

Chapter 10. Start now. Enjoy greater clarity of messaging, quality of insights and velocity of progress.

At each stage I offer tips, tools and templates developed over more than two decades of practice. Editable versions are also available in my online Clarity Hub – ClarityFirstProgram.com/ClarityHub. You receive one month's free membership to explore the MasterClasses, exercises, case studies and tools.

So let's lift the quality of thinking in your team's papers and presentations AND get your nights and weekends back.

I no longer spend up to 25 hours per weekend revising their papers and struggling through their emails. This has made a tremendous difference to my work and home life. My partner has commented on it, especially as we now have a six month old.

Sandip K, Executive Director, Strategy, Transformation, Major Capital and Digital, Regional Health Service

I prepared my analysis using a message map and my CEO said the leadership team had agreed that it was so clear, they could decide without meeting to discuss.

Charl-Stephan Nienaber, Manager, Strategy and Innovation, Provum Ventures

MasterClasses, tools and templates in the Clarity Hub

ClarityFirstProgram.com/ClarityHub
One month free

PART I

Lay strong foundations

CHAPTER 1

Think differently about your communication

Given you are reading this book, I assume you are interested in improving your team's communication skills and overall performance. Perhaps you are constantly on the lookout for ways to improve or perhaps your leaders have asked you to focus on this area.

You might even be thinking about hosting a workshop on writing or presentation skills.

In my experience, however, great writing and powerful presenting do not *cause* great communication. They are the *consequence* of great thinking.

This leads to clarity and confidence, which in turn leads to great writing and powerful presenting. When ideas are clear, papers and presentations are much more effective.

But how do you clarify thinking quickly and efficiently, especially in a busy and collaborative professional environment?

As one of my clients said:

The last thing I want is to polish each paper to perfection by constant iteration. I want a scalable 'system' that I can roll out across the organisation that supports better, faster collaboration.

So, let's lay the groundwork for you and your team so you can ...

▲ Focus more on decisions than on documents.
▲ Understand what drives poor paper quality.
▲ Set realistic targets for you and your team.
▲ Draw inspiration from others' experiences.

▲ Focus more on decisions than on documents

While central to many decision-making and governance processes, papers and presentations are a means to an end, not an end in themselves.

This idea is captured beautifully in a story my ex-McKinsey colleague Mike Sherman relayed to me when discussing this book:

My SingTel R&D analytics team worked extensively on the executive summary (or, message map) and building a tight deck that followed.

When we presented the summary to the division CEO, he responded with, 'Got it, this is a great idea, go ahead with it.'

Amy, the head of the team, sputtered, 'But don't you want to go through the deck?'

To which he replied, 'No. What you propose is clear, the support is clear, the next steps are clear; I have confidence the deck will support what you've just presented, I don't need to see the details.'

This blew her away – but after that she understood that investing time in the executive summary saved so much time down the road.

The three messages I want you to take from this are:

1. *Assuming the analysis is accurate, the quality of the messaging is what matters most.* If this is clear and insightful, you will inspire greater confidence in your stakeholders. The clarity and quality of insight show that you have done the work.

2. *This is a team effort.* As a leader you have perspective, skills and knowledge that your team members lack. You need to bring this into the process early so you and your team deliver maximum impact.

3. *It's both possible and helpful to map complex ideas on a single page.* It is reasonable to be skeptical at this point. You might think your communication is too complex to distill down to a single page. It's true that some complex pieces – such as a book like this – need multiple one-pagers for each section. The high-level messaging can still be (and was!) mapped on a page, however.

So, now I've put papers into perspective, let's look at what drives poor communication.

▲ Understand what drives poor paper quality

Why do managers and other stakeholders so routinely get out their red pen? Why is so much time spent playing 'ping-pong', batting papers to and fro in an attempt to squeeze out the message?

What drives so many executives to spend their nights and weekends reworking papers rather than getting the fast decisions they need? Here are four drivers that I see:

1. Insights are too hard to find.
2. Iteration relies on Track Changes.
3. Teams prepare papers with little understanding of the desired outcome.
4. Neither leaders nor teams are 'working at level'.

I'll now expand on each in more detail.

Insights are too hard to find

In my experience, problems with papers and presentations rarely result from an ability to use words or to craft sentences. Even if someone is not working in their first language, they are likely to perform at a fairly high level in their work. They couldn't do what they do if they weren't at least moderately proficient in the language. When at McKinsey in Hong Kong, this played out every day. Many – possibly most – people in the Hong Kong office in the 1990s did not have English as their first language. Yet they all performed at a very high level, even when their syntax or perhaps word choice wasn't 'native'.

The big question is why such focus is put on language ability, when this is not where the value lies. The value is in the ideas being conveyed.

I think this is because when we read someone's communication, words, sentences and formatting are *what we see*. If these aren't perfect, we worry that the insights aren't there. The real problem, however, is that *we can't find the ideas*.

To help you think about how this impacts your team's communication, I have named four common problems that I see. See if any of these resonate with you:

▲ *The wafer:* Ideas are loosely connected and light on detail. The paper does not provide sufficient detail to be convincing.

▲ *The Easter egg hunt:* Insights are buried in a disorderly slew of information. This forces the reader to hunt for the insights.

- *The Agatha Christie:* Insights are saved for the end, requiring the reader to work their way through the author's thinking process before the big reveal.
- *The miss:* The paper has a potentially strong narrative but addresses the wrong issues, even if those covered are technically accurate.

Think about the most recent papers you have either written or reviewed. Did any of these problems arise? If not, what problems did you see?

Iteration relies on Track Changes

I wonder if you dislike Track Changes as much as I do?

Passing a draft from person to person who adds comments or tweaks using Track Changes is a strategy that keeps everyone iterating in the weeds, especially when teams use it too early in their process. It also leads to many (many) unnecessary iterations full of comments that focus on minutiae.

Ask yourself, how many rounds of edits do you and your team take to land the final one?

Although this is a little extreme, I have seen clients draft 60+ versions of 10-page papers before landing their final version. More commonly, I see five to 10 iterations.

Either way, the time sink is unbelievable in relation to the gains.

I have also had people in my workshops yelp when they realise why their papers were rejected multiple times despite many, many iterations before each presentation.

In one instance, I was working with a group of mining engineers who realised their paper was repeatedly rejected because it answered the wrong question.

No matter how beautiful that paper was, it was never going to land with leaders until that question 'clicked'. Once they clarified the question they needed to answer, they could easily answer it.

This and many other teams I have worked with struggled because they were using a variation of a process I call the Chain of Pain. Typically, each person in the chain tracks their changes rather than providing a high-level contribution.

I have yet to work with a team who doesn't either groan or laugh in embarrassment when I explain it. Here's how it works:

1. Someone requests a paper.
2. Someone writes a paper, most likely going to some trouble to make the prose elegant and the charts better than just presentable.
3. They then send the draft around to peers and stakeholders for their input.

Here stakeholders focus on minutiae because they can't see the big picture. They make comments such as (and I quote), 'bit contradictory', 'bit vague', 'lovely word but the manager would call that jargon' (see below).

4. Eventually the author gets the paper back, fixes typos and sends it to you for review with little sense of ownership of the message or the document.

You're then asked to review this multi-edited paper.

What's the bet that you take one look at the draft and realise you can't do a 'quick flick' review?

You need to focus for a good chunk of time to digest the material so you can provide useful suggestions.

This will typically occur late at night or weekends and too often lead you to redraft the whole thing.

~~Track Changes keeps everyone in the weeds~~

 Mary
Will need to provide a couple of examples.

 Fred
Lovely word, but jargon?

 Mary
This needs some context. eg – while this work is via multiple initiatives, this is not reflected and tracked as HRIs in the RIS.

 Mary
Which time? Think Kylie mentioning the 3Q20 deadline to operationalise?

 Fred
Bit contradictory. First line says significant work is performed vs significant work remains.

 Mary
Bit abrupt?

Teams prepare papers with little understanding of the desired outcome

When working with teams, I begin by asking some benchmarking questions so I can measure what changes during our time together.

One question relates to a team's view of the quality of the briefings they receive before preparing papers. They frequently comment that these briefings are light and late.

Have you wondered how much time your team spends guessing what should be included in papers before they start preparing them? Sometimes they delay starting because they aren't sure of the real purpose behind the communication, others because they are not sure what information to include.

Whatever the reason, it's less efficient than it could be and results in more rework for you as you put the information in context.

What if you could cut that time it takes you and the team to iterate by a third or more? My data suggests that is imminently doable and possibly conservative. You may be able to halve the total time sink – while also delivering greater clarity around higher-quality insights.

Neither leaders nor teams are 'working at level'

With all this in mind, you might wonder why papers are so often finalised under pressure, even if the early drafts are prepared well ahead of time.

When key insights are hard to find, you and other stakeholders often delay your contribution.

All involved scan a draft, realise it needs more than a quick review, and 'park it' until they have time to focus properly on the details. Everyone needs thinking time that doesn't come easily.

By the time you get to the document it's too late to do anything else but rewrite it.

Clients describe at least four reasons why they rework their team's communication. Do any feel familiar? Do you:

1. want to avoid imposing on the team's private time when reviewing communication out of hours?
2. need to get into the weeds to work out what is actually wrong with the paper, which inevitably leads to rewriting even if that wasn't your original intent?
3. worry the team doesn't have the ability to prepare papers on their own?
4. struggle to let go of doing the work yourself since your promotion?

If these resonate, you are not doing what Martin G Moore describes in his book *No Bullshit Leadership* as 'working at level'. You and your team are all working at least one level below where your employer expects you to be. And working in this way *limits the impact you and your team deliver.*

So, how big a deal is this for you and your team?

Think about what you and your team could be doing if you weren't iterating unnecessarily around papers.

My colleague Richard Medcalf explains in his book *Making Time for Strategy* that the single most important predictor of success is making use of what he calls 'strategic time'. By this, he means the amount of time you spend thinking and delivering on strategic initiatives rather than operational ones.

Every unnecessary minute you spend reworking your team's papers limits your ability to add strategic value to your organisation. You are not designing and delivering new initiatives that will propel your area or perhaps the whole organisation forward more quickly.

So while unpacking where the costs lie within this example, think also about the strategic cost for your own area. What could you do with a couple of extra hours each week?

Case study: Freeing up two hours per week for Deborah

Let's take Deborah, the head of occupational health and safety (OH&S) at the Australian division of a multinational corporation. She has a team of nine, all of whom contribute to or write whole board papers.

This means she helps them prepare a monthly OH&S update for the board as well as ad-hoc papers to answer their questions and make recommendations. They are also involved in two substantial projects that report to steering committees.

All in, Deborah's team prepares at least 38 material papers each year: a dozen routine updates to the board, two to three ad-hoc papers about their projects for the board and, conservatively, 24 papers for the steering committees (that is, one steering committee report per month per project).

For Deborah, reviewing all these papers takes up a chunk of time spread across the year that hides in the hurly burly of 'work'.

My data suggests that on average leaders review papers three to four times. These reviews take time. The first review typically takes longer than subsequent ones, but the overall contribution is still considerable.

So, let's calculate the average time sink for Deborah if the initial briefing for a five-page paper takes 30 minutes, the first review conservatively takes two hours and each subsequent one takes 45 minutes. This results in a conservative four hours per paper.

Spread that over 38 papers for the year and Deborah averages just over three hours per week briefing for and reviewing papers. This work isn't evenly spread, however, because deadlines coincide. So Deborah works nights and weekends.

This estimate ignores other important communication Deborah reviews before the team sends to auditors, suppliers or customers.

It also ignores at least four downstream realities. Poorly crafted papers lead to ...

1. Boards and steering committees asking too many questions, delaying decisions and requiring you to re-present on the same topic.
2. Meetings requiring extra time so participants can ask questions to help them understand the paper, even if they do reach a decision in the end.
3. The team taking more time than necessary to create a quality paper.

4. Your brand as manager being put at risk. You may need to do some fancy footwork to compensate for the lack of synthesis and flow alongside poorly crafted visuals.

Compare this with what my data reveals about what is possible when leaders work with their teams to shift the dynamic.

I see the total leader time spent on a paper review commonly drop to less than one hour: a 15-minute briefing to share the understanding of the desired outcome of the communication and the stakeholder environment, and two 15-minute reviews. Let's add some flex and say that comes to an hour total.

For Deborah, changing the way she sets up the paper preparation process gives her on average about two hours back every week.

In reality this plays out as fewer late nights and weekends.

The team also gets time back as they iterate less on major papers and presentations, on top of the trickle-down effect of the techniques improving smaller more frequent communication such as emails. And meetings with the board and steering committee are also often shorter, with less need for follow-up and presenting again.

While Deborah is enjoying the two extra hours (or more) injected into her week, the clarity and quality of the communication also materially lifts.

Where do you sit on this? What could you do with an extra two hours in your week?

▲ Set realistic targets for you and your team

So, where do you want to get to? What is realistic for you and your team? How aspirational do you want to be?

My hunch is that the single most important measure of improvement is the time you spend reworking important papers. The less you need to review, the better communication. Where the number and depth of reviews is falling, three factors will be in play. Here are the questions I use to test for each of these:

1. *Clarity:* Can you glean the core messages within 30 seconds of opening a paper or presentation?
2. *Quality:* How valuable are the insights?
3. *Velocity:* How quickly can you and your team clarify and convey powerful insights that drive quality decisions?

I will now bring those to life with examples alongside questions you can use to measure your team's progress.

Clarity: Can you glean the core messages within 30 seconds?

It helps to ask how easily the insights jump off the page so your audience can grasp them quickly. How easy are they to find in the paper, presentation, discussion, email or other communication form?

As one board director highlighted recently, she wants the messages to pop off the page so she can skim before deciding how to read it deeply.

So, ask yourself how often you can glean the message within 30 seconds of opening a paper. You can also apply this to emails and other communication too.

While clarity is critical, though, it's not enough. To quote one of my 'crustier' clients, the head of credit risk at a large bank:

The team can now craft much clearer messages, which is great. But how do we stop them putting 'rubbish' in the boxes?

This leads me to my next dimension: quality of insight.

Quality: How valuable are the insights?

Do your team's papers deliver significant value to the project, team or organisation? Do they connect some dots to offer a new idea that adds value to the strategy, returns or processes, or perhaps reduce risk?

This is where both the challenge and the opportunity lie.

In *A Whole New Mind*, best-selling author Daniel Pink argues synthesis is the 'killer app' in business in what he calls the new Conceptual Age. Pink highlights:

What's in greatest demand today isn't analysis but synthesis – seeing the big picture and crossing boundaries, being able to combine disparate pieces into an arresting new whole.

Or, more simply, the formula we used at McKinsey:

SYNTHESIS = SUMMARY + INSIGHT

Daniel Pink is right. Most people can summarise – but so can natural language processing tools such as ChatGPT, if given the right data set.

The real value we humans bring is to join the facts with our own insights about the organisational context.

So, to offer high-quality, valuable insights, a team needs to be technically strong and in touch with the commercial and stakeholder imperatives.

This means adopting a common strategy for tying together complex ideas to make them *seem simple*.

This brings me to my third ingredient: velocity.

Velocity: How quickly can your team clarify and convey powerful insights that drive quality decisions?

Colin Bryar and Bill Carr were members of Amazon's senior leadership team. Their excellent book *Working Backwards*, which describes Amazon's secret to success, provides many insights.

The principle of velocity was one of them.

Amazon has gone to great lengths to maintain velocity in all areas of its operations so it can continue to execute quickly on innovative business lines. Removing bottlenecks is central.

Thinking like this about the processes surrounding your major communication deliverables will also help you.

Imagine if board paper received 'minimal adjustments' at each layer of your organisation's approval chain. Even better, imagine the board approving the idea the first time it is presented.

A client from the supply chain team at a large retailer coined a term to describe this: the Gold Standard. Here's how it works.

An individual or a team prepares a one-page message map before socialising that page with stakeholders. This one-pager triggers constructive debate around the big-picture ideas and how they connect with the data.

By socialising this message map rather than a polished document, at least three important things happen:

1. Everyone can review the message map and respond quickly with constructive suggestions to refine the thinking. One CEO client tells me he spends about 15 minutes reviewing each one-pager before the team prepares the final paper or presentation. This is a fraction of the time he previously spent reviewing papers for the senior leadership team and the board.

2. Stakeholders are more willing and able to debate the ideas. When someone receives a full document that someone has obviously 'sweated over', they feel less comfortable having the debate. Doing so feels more like a 'correction' than a 'conversation'.

3. The team spends less time preparing prose and charts that not only turn out to be off point, but which are also hard to let go of. As soon as someone creates a chart or writes a section, they can find it hard to let go. They spend time trying to 'fit it in' rather than stepping back and looking at the overall message they need to convey.

4. The team spends more energy thinking about the issues that matter, and so do you.

All of this liberates you and your team from the awful game of 'red pen ping-pong' so you can focus on higher order activities.

My clients frequently see a 30 per cent lift in velocity when drafting papers and presentations. This impacts both team members and leaders. Some teams, such as those outlined in the next section, achieve materially more than that.

Before establishing some concrete goals for you and your team, let's be inspired by what is possible.

▲ Draw inspiration from others' experiences

I have hundreds of stories, but have chosen three that I hope will resonate.

Project management office cut paper prep time by 80 per cent

One project management office (PMO) in a large company shredded their preparation time for key presentations by 80 per cent, while consistently getting decisions after 15 minutes. Let me unpack that:

- ▲ *Before:* The team spent a collective 15 hours preparing for each fortnightly steering committee meeting. These meetings frequently took two to three hours and often led to more questions than decisions.
- ▲ *After:* They took two to three hours to prepare their messaging. This then led to a 15-minute discussion and a concrete decision.

Safety review cut from two hours to eight minutes

In another instance, a head of safety for a retailer changed the dynamic for his quarterly updates with the CFO. These meetings went from two hours of him answering clarification questions about his 60-page presentation to two questions that he answered in eight minutes.

He and the CFO then enjoyed a quality discussion around the safety status and strategy, rather than unpicking the detail of the past quarter's slips and trips.

Analyst report removed need for senior level meeting

A brand new strategy analyst for a retirement village company had investigated the key drivers of the company's poor performance, and needed to report his findings. He emailed the leaders with his high-level messaging as an executive summary, and attached a detailed PowerPoint detailing his findings against each performance driver.

He received a thank you email from the CEO who said, 'You have laid out the situation so clearly, we don't need to meet to discuss this. We can see what we need to do.'

So, six senior people each spent less time understanding the findings, and gained half an hour from not meeting. It also put my client, in a positive light with senior leaders. You and your team can do this too.

CHAPTER 2

Iterate fast and early around the top-line messaging

My Elevate framework below gets the best out of you and your team quick time. It allows you to inject your situational awareness, influence skills, business acumen and domain knowledge into the process early. This adds rocket fuel to your team's ability to quickly clarify and convey high-quality communication.

This book focuses on your role as leader and explains how you can set your team up to make their own contribution. My

companion book, *Engage*, introduces the team's role in line with this framework while also offering detailed case studies that bring the approach to life.

In this four-chapter section, I preview this process. I explain the importance of each step before explaining how each one works in the coming chapters. I explain why it helps to:

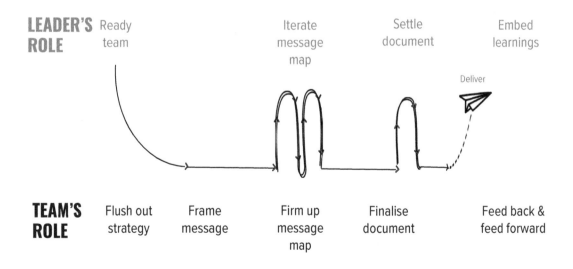

LEADER'S ROLE — Ready team — Iterate message map — Settle document — Embed learnings — Deliver

TEAM'S ROLE — Flush out strategy — Frame message — Firm up message map — Finalise document — Feed back & feed forward

Chapter 3: Ready your team so they know why they need to engage senior leaders on the required paper or presentation. This sets the team up to

a. flush out the communication strategy before writing anything
b. frame the messaging using patterns as a quick-start.

Chapter 4: Iterate the message map so you can provide fast feedback on their high-level messaging before the communication becomes a runaway train. You will collaborate with the team to quickly firm up the messaging using the one-page message map as a thinking tool that sets them up to prepare a document for you to review close to the due date.

Chapter 5: Settle the document to be confident in the final deliverable. Mostly, this will be a 'tick and flick', rather than a time-consuming review.

Chapter 6: Embed the learnings from both the process and the presentation so you and the team can all continuously improve.

▲ Ready your team

Every executive I have worked with has commented on how much time it can take to work out what key papers will achieve. The distance between the author and the audience can be vast and bridging that gap feels like a dark art.

The issue, however, is more about process than art.

Understanding the commercial reality behind a paper and being crystal clear about the associated outcome is essential for teams if they are to prepare a paper that is on point.

So, instead of leaving the team to work out what is required on their own, or with colleagues who are equally in the dark, I encourage you to schedule a briefing session as soon as you can.

This sets them up to and the team shift from 'here's what we need to talk about' to 'here's what we need to say to achieve a very specific outcome'.

Let me drive this home by first sharing two contrasting examples, before I step through the Elevate framework in the coming chapters.

Luke and Matt illustrate what *not* to do

Luke bumped into Matt, the CEO, in the hallway and the subsequent conversation went a bit like this.

Matt says, 'Great I caught you, Luke. Could you pull together a paper for next month's board meeting to update the board on your data analytics project? The Chair has been asking questions and wants to know where it is up to.'

Luke agrees and scurries off to his next meeting, as Matt also races toward his.

However, a significant disconnect in expectations exists that will cost them both.

Luke walks away pleased about getting airtime with the board, and thinking he should describe all the work he and his team have been doing.

Matt walks away looking forward to engaging the board in increasing its investment in data analytics for the coming year. He is particularly keen to make sure the board fully grasps the potential for understanding their customers more deeply to support more powerful marketing efforts the following year.

Perhaps, on the surface, this might not seem significant. Perhaps Luke could excite the board by describing all the 'fun things' he and his team are working on. However, Luke could help further Matt's agenda if he understood more about the commercial objective. It would help more still if Matt explained to Luke that the new chair isn't sold on the current data strategy and is being heavily influenced by the new director of sales, who has a very different strategy in mind.

I share this example to drive home how central your role is in briefing your team with great clarity.

I also want to highlight another aspect of this missed opportunity. It is tempting to keep your briefing light because you haven't yet had a chance to think through the strategy yourself. By involving the team early and setting them up to ask good questions, they help you clarify your own thinking more quickly and easily than if you had done so alone.

Let me also offer a polar opposite example so you can see the possibilities for you and your team.

Energy analysts showcase a better way

A group of analysts working for an energy company was astounded at how a strong initial briefing lit a match under their ability to pitch their business case. At the end of their one-hour planning session, they were clear how to make two years of analysis and research relevant to their leadership team.

The team had a clear understanding of what the stakeholders were looking for and a draft message map that they could flesh out. Together they had selected one of my favourite patterns, which I will share in coming chapters.

Once they had filled in the details, their leader approved it without adjustment. They then each worked on different sections to create a paper that aligned with the message map.

They were delighted to tell me that their (big) proposal was accepted after only about 10 minutes discussion at the senior leadership team (SLT) meeting.

The SLT was persuaded by the pre-read and had few questions.

I understand this isn't always as easy as it sounds, so I offer concrete strategies to help in the coming chapter.

For now, I want you to focus on how much faster and easier it is for your team to prepare papers when they understand who they are *really* for and what they need to achieve. Similarly, I am confident you will enjoy how much faster it is for you to review these papers too.

▲ Iterate around the one-page message map

Once the team has laid out their messaging as a one-pager, it becomes easier to provide quick and constructive input into the messaging before everyone invests heavily in a lengthy paper or presentation.

These one-pagers help you and the team fine-tune your messaging by doing at least three things. They

1. focus everyone on your main message
2. push you all to think harder
3. help clarify *and* convey your message.

I'll now unpack each of these to explain.

Message maps focus everyone on your main message

As a CEO from an Australian retailer said:

Do you mean I can ask everyone to prepare their one-pagers a week before the SLT or board meeting and then spend just 15 minutes reviewing each one?

I can block off a couple of hours and go through them all and pass back my feedback that quickly?

This approach gave him time to provide feedback and re-review where needed.

Message maps make this possible by prioritising three elements:

1. A short introduction that is less than 15 per cent of the whole document. Board members and senior leaders commonly complain that they dislike screeds of background at the start of a paper, so keep this short.

2. One single, short message that synthesises the entire message. If your audience only reads one sentence, this is it.

3. Two to five supporting points organised logically, using either a grouping or deductive structure. Here I combine logic and synthesis to draw out the insights, so they are easy to convey.

The map encourages you to work visually so you focus on the relationships between the ideas, rather than getting lost in screeds of prose or PowerPoint pages.

Working visually to clarify and then convey the relationships between the ideas within this message map is key. Here is a high-level skeleton to illustrate.

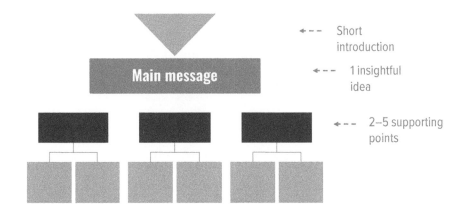

Short introduction

1 insightful idea

2–5 supporting points

Message maps push you all to think harder

Message maps are quite different from a document 'format' or 'template' that offers a list of topics to discuss. The map helps draw out the insights from your material rather than offering 'buckets' to throw ideas in.

As one of my McKinsey colleagues from years ago said:

This structure is a bit like an insight engine. The rules that underpin it help us tease out the message.

Whether preparing a high-stakes email that runs to half a page or a book like this one, you can use your one-pager to visualise the relationships between your ideas before preparing your communication. This means that even for a lengthy communication, you have a single A4 (or letter) page with your high-level thinking. For something as long as this book, I add sub-pages for each chapter that allow me to order the lower-level ideas.

I don't, however, do what one of my engineering clients did. Here's how they said they map their ideas:

You said to map our ideas onto a one-pager. We have been really good at doing that. We just decided that A4 was too small, so we went to A1 paper and used 4-point font.

This made me laugh. It was a fabulous solution even if missing the point entirely!

By limiting yourself to working on one small sheet of paper with a minimum of 10-point font, you're forced to summarise and synthesise.

You can 'cover everything' at a high level, but not include every little detail. You must put your ideas into a hierarchy, removing anything that does not support the main point.

Simply getting 'everything onto a single page', however, is not enough. In isolation, that will leave you iterating again and again to slowly rise above the detail to improve the expression. This strategy usually still requires your decision-makers to read from the beginning to the end to work out what you actually mean.

Instead, I encourage you to use a structured approach to thinking through the issues so you can distill and deliver powerful insights clearly and quickly. Let's now look at how to do that.

Message maps help clarify *and* convey your message

The diagram overleaf gives you a sense of what this message map looks like for a fairly complex recommendation. I will explain more deeply how it works in coming pages. For now, it helps to know what a real example looks like.

You can see there is room on the left side for a brief introduction, one single overarching message and then, on the right, three supporting points. Each of those points has a small number of high-level supports also. You can also see room for a very short headline at the top of the slide.

You can download a blank one along with the rest of my PowerPoint planner from the Clarity Hub Toolkit. (ClarityFirstProgram.com/ClarityHub).

Now I have introduced the basic structures, let's discuss how to use these one-pagers to create a paper or presentation.

▲ Settle the document by confirming the messaging and the document match

Once the message map is locked down, the team will prepare the document. The key is to make sure the integrity of the messaging is retained. The more settled the message map is before you turn it into a document, the easier this process will be. If it's not fully settled, ideas will evolve further as the team prepares the document, muddying the messaging.

Knowing when to swap from message map format to working in the document is a bit of an art. Although experience is likely the best tutor, the longer you wait the easier the transition will be.

Naturally, the more complex the paper and stakeholder group, the harder it is to get this right. So, I encourage you and the team to practice on shorter, lower-risk communication while, of course, not ignoring opportunities presented by a good challenge.

Either way, do your best to match the hierarchy of the messaging in the map with the hierarchy of the messaging in the document.

This will also make things easier for whoever presents it. The structure of the messaging will be crystal clear for everyone.

Meeting regulatory requirements requires us to transition all 105 legacy reports into the case system by the end of this financial year. We have now reviewed the associated work plans and received updated estimates.

We are now ready to share those estimates with you along with potential ways forward.

What are you suggesting?

Delivering the 105 reports means either investing $1.2m to $2m more over the coming two years or renegotiating requirements with the regulator.

Despite stress testing all budgets, we can't transition all 105 regulatory reports within the agreed $2m budget this financial year.

This means we need to make trade-offs when finalising the project workplans.

Therefore, we ask you to advise which tradeoffs we can make.

Updated estimates for database came back at $2m, which is 2.5 x the original budget due to more comprehensive scoping.

Budgets for other aspects of the work have not materially changed.
- Workflow remains same.
- API linking ditto.
- Operational teams ditto.

Work required for reports identified since June last year has not been factored in.

We could meet the scope by spending $1.2m to $2m more over the coming two years.
- We could deliver everything in FY23 with $1.2m more during FY23, or
- We could deliver some in FY23, some in FY24 with $2m or more in total.

We could renegotiate scope or time with the regulator.
- We could limit the scope and deliver only the top 70 reports by FY23 (fix existing 36, do another 35ish) within the current budget, or
- We could seek agreement from the regulator to further extend the project and deliver all at a later date.

Decide whether to spend more ...
- Decide whether to increase funding by $1.2m for FY23.
- Decide whether to budget $2m more for the project in total and roll into next year.

Decide whether to renegotiate ...
- Decide whether to pitch the regulator to accept the top 70 reports as adequate for FY23.
- Decide whether to seek extensions.

▲ Embed the learning

This is the easiest step to ignore but I can't stress its importance enough. If you want your team to write papers that senior leaders can approve without adjustment, you need to hear what worked and what didn't.

Your team may or may not be in the meeting where their paper is presented. Even if they are, they are unlikely to catch all the nuances given they don't have the same history with the decision-makers that you do. Equally, their fresh eyes and questions may help you better understand these decision-makers.

Having now provided a helicopter view of the way forward, in the following chapters I help you lift your own skills before outlining how you can elevate your team's abilities.

PART II

Lift out of the detail

CHAPTER 3

Ready your team

When helping your team improve their communication, the last thing you want to do is get in their way.

As a leader this is easy to do, simply by leaving your briefing too late, or providing one that is too scant. The team will then spend hours, and sometimes days, trying to work out what a paper or presentation aims to achieve. Let's avoid that by briefing them early and well.

This involves five steps:

- ▲ Plan your briefing so you have the right people and set the right expectations.
- ▲ Clarify the desired outcome so the team understands what this communication needs to deliver.
- ▲ Understand the audience deeply, to help the team target their messaging.
- ▲ Iterate to refine your communication strategy to really 'nail it'.
- ▲ Pick a pattern to help the team structure the high-level messaging.

I share examples throughout to bring the approach to life, beginning with simpler and more general examples.

I do this to introduce the concepts simply, without the risk of an example getting in the way of your conceptual understanding.

You will soon see that although the concepts are quite simple, they require practice if you are to squeeze out the very last drop of insight from your information.

▲ Plan your briefing

Briefings can vary widely according to the complexity of the material and the ability and availability of your team. I offer three ideas here to help you get the most out of these sessions. Let's begin.

Brief the team as early as you can

You will, of course, be mindful of your own workload and priorities as well as those of the team in scheduling this briefing. However, I encourage you to delay less than you might.

This has at least two benefits. It provides a longer runway and also kick starts the thinking process sooner for all of you. It allows you all to use both focused time and what is called *diffused time* to flush out the messaging. Focused time occurs when you are actively thinking about something. Diffused time occurs when you are doing something else, but allowing the ideas to marinate. Think of it as shower time or dog walking time. Without extra effort, these relaxed times are often when ideas click into place.

Starting earlier opens the door for your team to ask questions that help you clarify your own thinking sooner.

Doing this in no way diminishes the value you bring; rather it magnifies the quality of thinking and problem solving you and your team deliver.

Invite everyone who will be involved in preparing the paper

I recommend inviting everyone who will have a role in preparing the paper to this planning session, including junior team members who may only focus on discrete sections. You may also think expansively around the five Es:

▲ *Effort:* Do they have sufficient capacity or interest to contribute right now?

▲ *Elevation:* Do they have sufficient visibility of the strategic environment to help link your narrative to the broader business objectives?

You may bring sufficient visibility on your own, or equally, you may bring someone senior into the session to share their perspective.

It could be the person who commissioned the paper, someone who owns the relevant business strategy or someone who knows the stakeholder group well.

- *Evaluative ability:* Do they bring fresh eyes and raw intelligence that may help the team think from first principles?
- *Experience:* Do they bring practical, hard-earned wisdom?
- *Expertise:* Are they familiar with the problem or have a usefully different perspective? Most likely they will have been working on the issue.

In briefing the whole team, you will increase the chances of clarifying a message that hits the right notes with less effort from you all.

Tailor the briefing to match your needs and the team's abilities

My clients say these sessions vary from a 15-minute 'here's what you need to know' chat to an in-depth hour or so working through the strategy and framing the high-level messaging.

You will no doubt vary your contribution according to the specific team members and the nature of the challenge. Naturally, the bigger the gap between them and the task, the more deeply you will be involved. Here are three thoughts on how to calibrate your involvement:

- *Routine papers such as updates:* Set these up once and tweak the basic structure only when the nature of the work or key stakeholders change. Delegate oversight to a 'champion' with strong communication and coaching potential to save your involvement for where it matters.
- *Updates where something has changed:* Updates commonly move away from being 'just an update' toward a recommendation for changing the forward strategy. You may need to be more involved in these discussions than when preparing an 'all is well' update.
- *Ad-hoc and high-stakes papers:* These may require you to roll your sleeves up. If unsure how much help the team needs, I recommend working with the team up front on both the communication strategy and message map to give them the best chance of quickly nailing the message. This will of course require more up-front involvement from you, but is more constructive for both you and the team as it will reduce rework later.

Once you have run a few of these briefings you will find a rhythm that suits you all. I'll now share the key things to discuss at each one.

▲ Clarify your desired outcome

Understanding the commercial reality behind a paper and being crystal clear about the associated outcome is central to you and your team performing 'at level'. If your team understands what this communication must deliver, they are more likely to deliver it. You are also less likely to then spend your nights and weekends reworking it.

The first step is to ensure your team is clear on the desired outcome for the communication. I'll now explain how to do this and illustrate with an example.

Approach: Use a tightly structured statement to gain extreme clarity around your desired outcome

This is where much of the deep thinking takes place. In my coaching sessions, the message map comes together quite quickly after the initial thinking about the outcome and the audience is clear. Gaining that clarity can be a bit like peeling an onion, though, where you need to layer into the real situation and the real goal.

This single sentence frames the thinking about what will go into the communication. This statement is not included in the document itself, but used to frame the thinking that does go into the document.

I encourage you to be highly specific when completing the following statement:

> As a result of this **specific piece of communication** *[name it]* I want **my audience** *[name the top person or perhaps top three people who will be pivotal to the decision and/or could derail the implementation]* to **know**, **think** or **do** ... *[name the action you want your audience to take; for example, 'agree', 'decide' or 'understand'].*

Pushing for extreme clarity around the three bold variables turns light bulbs on. You and your team need to drill deeply into which piece of communication you are referring to, which audience member will have the most sway over the decision and what specific outcome you need.

Creating clarity around this requires you to scan your environment for clues that your team cannot see. You have greater visibility of the strategic and stakeholder environments and most likely also either more experience, stronger business acumen or both.

Here are some questions to ask yourself about the outcome you seek so you can feed that into your discussions with your team:

1. Who asked for this communication?
   a. If a routine report, go beyond 'we just do this' to ask yourself what value it delivers. Why is this report really needed? Who uses it? How does it help them? Why?
   b. If an ad-hoc paper, go beyond who asked you for it to clarify who initiated the request in the first instance.
2. Why did they ask for it?
   a. What is concerning or exciting them?
   b. Is there a gap in what is currently being done about the issue and what they think is needed?
   c. What has changed internally or externally that has triggered their curiosity about this issue?
3. How do these issues align with the strategic direction for your team, division, organisation or perhaps industry?

Let me illustrate how this works by working through a paper seeking leadership support for a regulatory project.

Example: Re-scoping a derailed project

I chose this example because it is so delightfully real. Tightly designed scopes for well-understood and clearly defined tasks supported by aligned stakeholder groups teach us less. So in this example, I highlight how you can use these concepts in (hopefully relatably) messy situations.

The 'fix these reports now' project was about meeting a regulator's requirement that a bank improve the quality of 105 customer reports. These reports needed to accurately reflect the viability of customer accounts that had changed since their inception.

Customers might have, for example, swapped from one type of loan to another or added more loans or credit cards. These changes alter their aggregate position with the bank. The team needed to deliver better operational workflows, more efficient case management and more accurate reporting on the status of these customer accounts. This in turn gave greater clarity about the bank's overall financial position.

The project had not made good progress over the year before my client was brought in as manager. He was asked to 'fix it' with $2 million. Success, at a minimum, would be replacing the 105 legacy reports with functioning, automated reports that enabled the bank to know if customer accounts were profitable or not with significantly less manual processing.

His first task was to review the current status before making a recommendation to leadership. He found that despite $3 million being spent over the past year, the team had produced only 33 *unusable* reports. The reports did not, for example, factor in duplicates. This led to overstating problems by up to 70 per cent.

So, my client had a condensed time frame to deliver 105 *usable* reports. To add to the challenge, the IT team had been unavailable over his first three months in the role.

In thinking through your desired outcome and audience for a paper like this, you might focus on leaders with the most interest in and influence over this project. This will likely be gleaned from experience, your understanding of each member's roles and responsibilities, their past behaviour when budgets are challenged and what they have said about the topic in previous meetings.

In that case, your statement might be something like this:

As a result of this **paper**, I want the **executive** to **approve another $1.2 million in funding so we can complete the 105 reports on time at the end of this financial year**.

This draft offers a useful starting point. You will see, though, that as the audience is better understood, it can be finessed further to be more accurate and more useful.

This draft initially felt like the right ask given the project manager's understanding of the looming 'mortgage cliff'. A large number of home loans would soon expire, leading borrowers to renegotiate at a likely unaffordable higher rate.

His view was that the project needed more money and focus to reduce the impact of significant interest rate hikes that would lead borrowers to change their loans. These changes would then need to be manually updated in the current legacy reports that help the bank understand its position ... unless the project succeeded in updating the reports ASAP.

As you will soon see, his view morphed as together we better understood the audience. This revised view was then reflected in a revised outcome statement.

▲ Understand your audience deeply

The next step is to clarify who your audience *really* is. This may be obvious but sometimes it's not. I find it helpful to brainstorm their names and then organise them against a framework that points to who has the most interest in the issue and who has the most influence over it.

Once you have identified the most influential stakeholders, unpacking their mindset around your topic can be helpful.

I suggest classifying their attitudes in relation to your specific message according to one of the four following stances:

▲ *Champions:* Ardent supporters, likely to 'win' from your proposal, and so also likely to help you get it across the line.

▲ *Objectors:* Quite the opposite to champions. They may have one of three concerns – that they are likely to 'lose' from the changes, are philosophically opposed or perhaps don't understand them.

▲ *Neutral:* Unconcerned about the proposal, may have confidence in whatever you propose or believe that your proposal is one of many equally useful solutions.

▲ *Advocates:* Intellectually supportive but unlikely to go out of their way to support you. They can see the advantages, but most likely they are largely unaffected by your proposal.

As you will see, this work may also influence your recommendation itself. Understanding stakeholder issues and concerns helps clarify both what is needed and what is possible.

On the coming page I share how my client and I sketched out the top five stakeholders for this narrative, using the PowerPoint Planner from the Clarity Hub Toolkit.[1]

---

1   ClarityFirstProgram.com/ClarityHub

#1 Clarify your desired outcome

As a result of this paper, I want the executive to approve more funding either as another $1.2 million for this year or seek to carry over into FY 24.

#2 Understand your audience

Head of Projects: Has been taking resources away and providing them to other people recently. Is in a tight spot as juggling many 'important' projects with diminished resources. Fearful of being blamed for inadequate delivery of phase 1 of the project.

Head of IT and Data: Happy to continue working on the project assuming it's given the right level of priority and doesn't over stretch their team. Likes that the new strategy doesn't drip feed random reports to them but rather relies on a clear, well-scoped plan up-front.

Head of Consumer Mortgages: Relieved to have someone coming in who can sort this project out. Has offered every kind of support needed. Trusts the new project manager to deliver. Needs to engage with regulator, so is embarrassed about lack of delivery so far. Rates this project as #1 in her area.

Head of Risk and Compliance: Very keen to get this project completed ASAP given the regulator commitment.

Operations team that provides the reports: Needs the new, more efficient reports but struggling to find capacity to implement them. They are resource constrained and have been told not to change their processes as 'solutions are coming'. Currently under cost-out pressure while facing increased workload due to the extra work required to prepare reports using the older manual process.

#3 Map your stakeholders

Degree of influence over the decision

Powerful influencers

Head of IT: *Advocate – likes that it is well scoped*

Head of Projects: *Advocate – assuming they are given resources and can avoid taking the blame for lack of delivery so far*

Others

Decision-makers

Head of Consumer Mortgages: *Champion – embarrassed that the project has run over so far*

Head of Risk: *Champion – needs to keep regulator on side*

Less powerful influencers

Operations team: *Champions for bigger budgets*

Project team: *Neutral*

Degree of interest in the issue

▲ Iterate to refine your communication strategy

Now you have defined your desired outcome in a general sense and learned more about your stakeholders, it's time to iterate.

Continuing the same example, thinking more about the stakeholders makes it clear that the primary decision-makers were the Heads of Consumer Mortgages and Risk, rather than the whole executive group. So, my client and I refined the desired outcome accordingly.

Here is the original draft for reference:

> As a result of this **paper**, I want the **executive** to **approve another $1.2 million in funding so we can complete the 105 reports on time at the end of this financial year**.

We then iterated to be more specific about who the critical stakeholders were, as follows:

> As a result of this **paper**, I want the **Heads of Consumer Mortgages and Risk** to **approve another $1.2 million in funding so we can complete the 105 reports on time at the end of this financial year**.

This is as far as we went at this stage, but as we thought more about it, we further refined the 'ask' to better reflect the roles and responsibilities of key stakeholders, along with their perceived appetite for investment. We redrafted as follows:

> As a result of this **paper**, I want the **Heads of Consumer Mortgages and Risk** to **decide whether to spend more to deliver the 105 reports in full over the coming two years or to renegotiate requirements with the regulator**.

Iterating around the desired outcome is central to confirming the stakeholder management strategy.

If, for example, you realised that the decision-maker – let's choose the Head of Consumer Mortgages in this instance – was adamant that no more budget was available, you need to think hard about how to proceed.

Would you set up a one-on-one with them to brief them on the delivery challenges to stress test that point of view?

Would you go to the Head of Risk and stress test the possibility of extending the regulator's deadline?

If so, what would your desired outcome be for each of these conversations?

The outcome of either one of these conversations would bring you back to think again about the desired outcome for your executive committee meeting.

So, you need to iterate back and forth between the different stages in the process as your thinking matures. For now, though, we move on to the next stage.

Once you have clarified your understanding of your outcome and audience, it is much easier to land your messaging.

The trick for you as leader now is to decide how far you go along this path with your team and how far you ask them to go alone before they iterate back to you.

This is something I can't answer for you, but I can share some ideas to help you map the message with the team if you judge that is right.

▲ Pick a pattern to help your team structure the message

If you are familiar with design thinking, this technique for prototyping your story might not seem so strange. If not, then sit tight: you will enjoy it!

Having helped leaders engage senior decision-makers for a couple of decades, I have identified 10 common story patterns that are ideally suited for complex senior stories.

These jump-start your thinking, removing the need for you and the team to start from a blank page.

I'll now unpack that for you at a high level. These patterns:

- ▲ help prototype your message early
- ▲ support a wide range of outcomes
- ▲ offer flexibility within a framework
- ▲ help your message 'click'.

I introduce the patterns here to give you a bird's eye view of the process. I also offer a how-to guide and case studies for each pattern in my companion book, *Engage*.

Patterns help prototype your message early

Given you no longer need to start with a blank sheet, I encourage you to think through your strategy and then prototype – or hack – what your narrative might look like against a couple of promising patterns. In playing with a couple of examples – potentially more than a couple if your thinking is still unclear – you can quickly stress test your messaging.

Interestingly, I have found that doing this also helps firm up the strategic direction. When looking at a skeleton story, you can't always articulate what is working or not; but, you often know that something either is or is not right. This insight nudges you to think harder about what is really needed.

Laying some skeletons out against each other is a fast and effective way to tighten the strategy, frame up the story and reduce the risk of preparing whole papers or presentations that must be rewritten – or, worse, whole papers or presentations that are written and then rejected because they miss the point.

You may also find my Pattern Picker a useful adjunct to this process. It guides you through a decision tree to identify promising patterns. I include a simple version in this book and a more nuanced version leading to more sophisticated patterns inside the Clarity Hub.

Whichever strategy you use, hold back on preparing the document until you are comfortable with the message. Junking pages and pages of elegant PowerPoint is hard, even when they no longer have a place in the story. So let's reduce the chance that you and your team prepares them in the first place.

Patterns support a wide range of outcomes

I have been experimenting with patterns for many years to help my clients clarify their thinking faster.[2] It seems to be easier to react to something than start from scratch and so I have codified the commonalities between the thousands of papers I have helped clients prepare.

The 10 patterns I am about to share with you result from that experimentation. I've found this set to be well suited to communicating with senior leaders and boards.

---

2   Gerard Castles and I published seven useful patterns in our book *The So What Strategy* in 2017.

10 patterns to help you quickly structure your messaging to align with most desired outcomes

I will now introduce my top 10 patterns and then follow with my Pattern Picker process that helps you decide which one (or ones) to test. I have drawn these up below with the main message at the left before sketching out the top-line supporting points for each. You will see two basic shapes for these points. One, a grouping, offers a list of independent points to support the message and the other, a deductive chain, builds a case for action.

For informing: Nike and Nugget

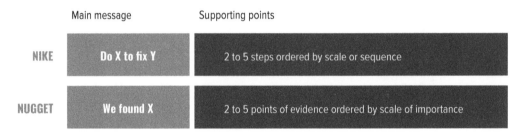

For building or maintaining confidence when 'all is well'

For delivering strategies: Golden, Make the Case and Oh Dear

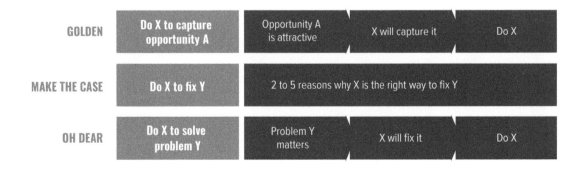

For discussing options: Short List and This or That

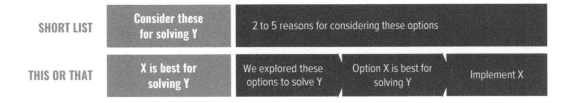

For recommending improvements: Change Tack and Top Up

The Pattern Picker links your desired outcome and narrative structure

You will notice that these patterns are heavily weighted toward persuasion.

I find that in many instances where clients assume their audience 'just needs to know', they are missing something. This is especially so for updates. I always dig more deeply to ask why they need to know and, in doing so, frequently unearth the real need. I encourage you to do the same.

In using the Pattern Picker on the coming page, you first lean heavily on the desired outcome. This shapes the type of message that will resonate with your audience and then achieve the outcome you need.

I have kept the options simple. I am confident that in most cases you will work out which of these options suits your situation best. If, however, you need more nuance, try my Pattern Picker from the Clarity Hub[1].

---

1   ClarityFirstProgram.com/ClarityHub

Pattern Picker Framework

1 – CLARIFY OUTCOME	2 – REVIEW POTENTIAL MESSAGES	3 – FIND MESSAGE		4 – FRAME MESSAGE
I need my audience to ...	To achieve that I must explain ...	... then pick a pattern		... and structure it
> Action > Endorse > Implement > Support	**Action plans** How to proceed	Nike	**Do X to fix Y**	2 to 5 steps ordered by sequence or scale
> Know > Understand	**Findings** What analysis revealed	Nugget	**We found X**	2 to 5 points of evidence ordered by scale of importance
> Have confidence > Trust	**Updates** The status is green, project is going well	All is Well	**We are in good shape**	2 to 5 reasons why we are in good shape, ordered by task or time
> Agree > Approve > Change > Decide > Endorse	**Strategies** How to capture a new opportunity	Golden	**Do X to capture opportunity A**	Opportunity A is attractive, X will capture it, so do X
	How to solve a problem or capture an opportunity	Make the Case	**Doing X will fix Y**	2 to 5 reasons explaining why X is the right way to fix Y
	How to solve a problem that is new to your audience	Oh Dear	**Do X to solve problem Y**	Problem Y matters, but X will fix it, so do X
	Options Which options to evaluate	Short List	**Consider these for solving Y**	2 to 5 reasons to consider these options
	Best way to capture an opportunity or solve a problem	This or That	**Option X offers best approach**	We explored these options for solving Y, but option X is best, so implement X
	Improvements How to address an emerging opportunity or risk	Change Tack	**Make a change to reach goal**	Have made progress, but need to make a change to reach goal, so make a change
	How to succeed when you meet only some necessary criteria	Top up	**Top up to succeed at Y**	Succeeding at Y requires X, but we have only some of X in place, so top up

When you need to inform

Let's look at the key outcomes you might seek from your communication so you can double check you do *really* only need to inform. This is worth testing. In my experience, clients over index on 'inform' because they don't think deeply about what outcome they really need.

When informing, you are typically asking your stakeholder to do one of the following:

▲ *Action:* Undertake one or more tasks, where your audience needs little explanation as to why this action matters.

▲ *Implement:* Put something into effect where you explain what to do but the audience decides how to do it.

▲ *Support:* Help someone, potentially you, to undertake an activity without undertaking the activity themselves.

▲ *Know:* Be aware of something so your stakeholder can factor this knowledge into their thinking and action.

▲ *Note or Understand:* Fully appreciate something so your stakeholder can then use that understanding to decide or act.

When you need to persuade

When persuading, you are typically asking your stakeholder to do one of these seven things:

▲ *Agree:* To agree, regardless of their level of accountability or authority.

▲ *Approve:* To enable something they have accountability for to proceed.

▲ *Change:* To change the way something they have authority over is done.

▲ *Decide:* To choose a way forward for something they have authority over.

▲ *Endorse:* To publicly approve something that the stakeholder doesn't have accountability to deliver, but which relies upon their support.

▲ *Have or maintain confidence:* To believe you can deliver, largely based on positive past experience.

▲ *Trust:* To continue to support you, even where there may not be past examples of success.

Your organisation may have slightly different definitions. If so, adjust accordingly.

Once you are comfortable with the outcome you seek, feed this into the Pattern Picker to work out which structure is likely to suit your situation best.

Patterns offer flexibility within a framework

I've found patterns to be a terrific way to take full advantage of structured thinking techniques without being 'expert'.

By starting with a pattern, you can fairly quickly work out what you need to say. You can then check your draft against first principles to further tighten your thinking. I have three caveats, however.

Firstly, you will most likely not need to master all 10 patterns. You will return to your favourites that work best for your own situation.

Secondly, 'tweaking' the structures is risky if you deviate from first principles. These patterns work because they adhere to some relatively simple yet important rules of logic and synthesis. I'll introduce these in more depth in the next chapter.

Thirdly, although these are powerful short cuts that cover many, many situations, they may not be the only structures you ever use.

Once you are familiar with the underlying structuring principles, you can tweak the patterns to better suit your own needs. Sometimes this means merging various aspects of them or flipping them to the opposite direction.

For example, you might notice that the Oh Dear and Golden patterns on the page to the right are similar. Oh Dear starts introducing a new material problem whereas Golden begins with an attractive opportunity.

In creating these two variants, I 'flipped' the first point (the statement) from the classic negative Oh Dear beginning to a positive, to explain that we have a golden opportunity.

I've hosted workshops with my advanced students where we take on the idea of 'pattern flipping' as a thinking skills exercise to create new ones. With some practice, you will be able to do the same.

You can also short cut this process by using the Pattern Picker, which I'll introduce shortly or perhaps by using the more nuanced version from the Clarity Hub[3], when your situation is murkier than usual.

It helps you think through the nuances within your communication strategy, refine your desired outcome and tease out specifically the sorts of information your audience needs from you.

---

3   ClarityFirstProgram.com/ClarityHub

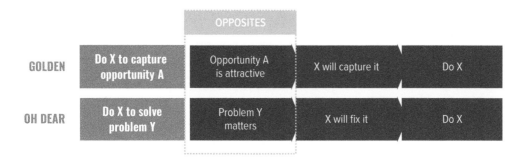

		OPPOSITES		
GOLDEN	Do X to capture opportunity A	Opportunity A is attractive	X will capture it	Do X
OH DEAR	Do X to solve problem Y	Problem Y matters	X will fix it	Do X

I now return to the 105 reports case study to show you how we used patterns to help our messaging 'click'.

Patterns help your message 'click'

So far we have thought through our desired outcome for the 105 reports story, refining our thinking about our own objective and which stakeholders are central to achieving that.

Once our desired outcome was clear, we started thinking about the structure of the paper. We could have worked bottom-up by laying out the facts and grouping and sorting our ideas to arrive at the structure.

But, we decided to try a pattern first, and marry that with our bottom-up understanding of the facts later.

I'll describe how we iterated together to find the high-level messaging before explaining the four steps we took to land the messaging.

We iterated to find the high-level messaging

We took a quick guess about what might work without being picky. We did this by focusing on the verb used in the outcome statement, matching that with the kinds of information we needed to convey and picking a pattern.

We then 'coloured the patterns in' with the information at hand, iterating to either improve that version or test a new one if our high-level skeleton didn't seem quite right.

In this example, we iterated around the high-level structure four times. This is a fairly common amount of hacking for a paper of this nature. We also used the hacking process to further refine our communication strategy.

In this situation, the refinements were important but not so great that we felt our overall path was wrong.

In some situations where our thinking is mature this 'hacking' process will involve just two rounds. In others we might do up to 10 rounds.

Lots of rounds signals that significantly more thinking is needed around both the strategy and the content to land your messaging.

Once the pattern clicks into place, I then move on to the next slide in the PowerPoint planner and flesh out the full message map.

I will now illustrate how we worked through this 'hacking' process for the 105 reports narrative, linking our desired outcome with the information key stakeholders needed to work out which pattern to try first.

We landed the messaging in four steps

Here is how we hacked our way to the structure for the 105 reports paper.

Let me first remind you of our understanding of the desired outcome when we began hacking:

> As a result of this paper, I want the Heads of Consumer Mortgages and Risk to **APPROVE** another $1.2 million in funding so we can complete the 105 reports on time at the end of this financial year.

We scanned the left-hand column of the Pattern Picker to find patterns for stories that require approval.

Given my client's feeling was that the team needed to lean into the problem and 'fix the reports' within the regulator's time frame, Top Up seemed like a good place to start.

Here's how we thought it through, numbering each attempt so it is easier for you to follow the diagram on page 48.

Step 1. Top Up quickly felt wrong. The first point, the statement, was not substantive enough and was known to the audience. It didn't belong below the main message. The top-line supporting points and those below them should only introduce ideas that are news.

Step 2. We quickly moved onto Oh Dear and kept iterating around that until we got pretty close in version three. You can see how our thinking firms up if you review the three 'hacks'.

- Our first 'go' was helpful for the wrong reasons. It enabled my client to vent his frustrations. When seeing the thoughts on paper, it became clear that it was indelicate, and unlikely to be persuasive.
- The second attempt was better, but still not right. The first main point, the statement was thin on substance and felt belligerent.
- The third re framed the problem so it was both constructive and strong. It also led to an important shift in the desired outcome, more accurately reflecting roles and responsibilities of everyone involved.

Here's what it became:

As a result of this paper, I want the Heads of Consumer Mortgages and Risk to **DECIDE** whether to spend more to deliver the 105 reports in full over the coming two years or to renegotiate requirements with the regulator.

Now the ideas had clicked it was time to add detail, so we moved to the one-page message map.

Step 3. We then further tweaked Oh Dear once we transitioned into the message map, tightening the messaging and elevating our synthesis. You can see quite a lift in the messaging quality from the hacked version to the final version.

Step 4. We used some of the ideas from our initial 'go' at Top Up to introduce the story. We did this because it seemed like a sensible place to start in that it introduced relevant information about the reports project that was known by the audience. Because it was known, it did not need detailed explanation.

As you will see, we deliberately avoided typing over each draft as we iterated, but kept them next to each other to allow for healthy discussion and debate.

I have laid this out on the coming page just as we did in real-time, adding colour coding to help you link our notes to the message map on the following page.

Once you have reviewed these, it's time to dive more deeply into message structuring.

We hacked four potential patterns before choosing Oh Dear Version 3

1 – Top up – The first point, the statement was known, so we moved it to the introduction (as you can see in the message map on the page to the right)

- [STATEMENT] Meeting regulatory requirements requires us to transition all 105 legacy reports into the case system
- [COMMENT] However, we need extra funding to deliver the 105 reports (fixed scope)
- [RECOMMENDATION] Therefore, we must review funding:
  - Funding flex
  - Schedule
  - Resources

2 – Oh Dear v1 – The statement was indelicate

- [STATEMENT] The reason the reports were not delivered over the past two years was that the scoping was inadequate
- [COMMENT] However, now we have accurate scoping, we can consider several tradeoffs that will enable us to deliver reports
- Therefore, consider tradeoffs

3 – Oh Dear v2 – Getting closer but the statement wqas too thin and felt belligerent

- [STATEMENT] We can't deliver the 105 reports within the current funding window (explain why not)
- [COMMENT] However, we can deliver some of the reports by making tradeoffs along two dimensions to proceed with the project:
  - Deliver everything in FY23 – Funding flex
  - Deliver some in FY23, some in FY24 – Schedule, scope FY23 flex and funding flex for FY24
- [RECOMMENDATION] Therefore, decide which tradeoffs to make

4 – Oh Dear v3 – Better tone, room to describe options in middle section

- [STATEMENT]: Despite testing all budgets, the 105 regulatory reports can't be delivered within the $2m budget during FY23 (explain why not – we have stress-tested the budgets)
- [COMMENT] However, we can deliver some of the reports by reprioritising funding in FY23 and FY24:
  - Deliver everything in FY23 with $1.2m more during FY23
  - Deliver some in FY23, some in FY24 with $2m or more in total
  - Deliver only the top 70 reports by FY23 (fix 36, do another 35ish)
- [RECOMMENDATION] Therefore, decide which tradeoffs to make:
  - Increase funding?
  - Pay more for the total project?
  - Accept the top 70 reports in FY23 is adequate?
  - Seek extensions from the regulator?

Meeting regulatory requirements requires us to transition all 105 legacy reports into the case system by the end of this financial year. We have now reviewed the work plans and received updated estimates.

The 'what' above emerged as from our initial pattern hacking. It comes from our first attempt with the Top Up pattern.

We are now ready to share those estimates with you along with potential ways forward.

What are you suggesting?

Delivering the 105 reports means either investing $1.2 million to $2 million more over the coming two years or renegotiating requirements with the regulator.

This main message emerged after the rest of the story came together. It offers a point of view, even though its not a decision in itself.

Despite stress testing all budgets, we can't transition all 105 regulatory reports within the agreed $2 million budget this financial year.	This means we need to make trade-offs when finalising the project workplans.	Therefore, we ask you to advise which tradeoffs we can make.
Updated estimates for database came back at $2m, which is 2.5 x the original budget due to a more comprehensive holistic scoping. **Budgets for other aspects of the work have not materially changed.** • Workflow remains same. • API linking ditto. • Operational teams ditto. **Work required for reports identified since June last year has not been factored in.**	**We could spend $1.2m to $2m more over the coming two years.** • We could deliver everything in FY23 with $1.2m more during FY23, or • We could deliver some in FY23, some in FY24 with $2m or more in total. **We could renegotiate scope or time with the regulator.** • We could deliver only the top 70 reports by FY23 (fix existing 36, do another 35ish) within the current budget, or • We could seek agreement from the regulator to further extend the project and deliver all at a later date.	**Decide whether to spend more ...** • Decide whether to increase funding by $1.2m for FY23. • Decide whether to budget $2m more for the project in total and roll into next year. **Decide whether to renegotiate ...** • Decide whether to pitch the regulator to accept the top 70 reports as as adequate in FY23. • Decide whether to seek extensions from the regulator. These supporting points use repetitive language to test that the ideas are parallel. We edit this out when transitioning into document format.

CHAPTER 4

Iterate the message using structured thinking principles

Message maps are the engine-room of this approach. They help us arrange our information into a tight structure that showcases the main message and the logic behind it.

They begin with a short introduction that primes an audience to be ready for our single, insightful main message. We then support that main message by organising our information logically.

Easy, right?

Superficially yes, but practically no.

Visualising your ideas into a hierarchy as below is hugely powerful. By understanding specifically how the ideas relate to each other in both the one-page message map and the final communication is key. Ensuring each idea tightly connects to the others is where the power lies.

I now explain how to power up your own communication. I encourage you to:

▲ Lean on structure to lift the quality of your messaging.

▲ SCORE the quality of your messaging.

▲ Review an example to see the difference between strong and weak.

▲ Structure the messaging for a communication of your own.

Let's dive in to each of these one by one.

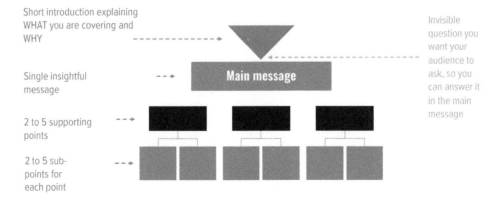

▲ Lean on structure to lift the quality of your messaging

In the coming section I break the structure into parts to help you create and evaluate each one.

I explain how the introduction quickly draws your audience toward your main message. It avoids offering lots of history and background, but rather readies your audience for your single, overarching and insightful point of view.

I then offer four different levels of 'idea' so you can decide how much value your main message needs to deliver.

Lastly, I explain how to structure the supporting points two ways to round out that message and prepare a paper or presentation that is both clear and compelling. Let's dig in.

The introduction quickly draws your audience toward your main message

Many papers and presentations offer too much background before getting to the main point. I see many offer details that they think the audience needs to know in order to understand their main point.

I challenge that idea, and instead encourage you to quickly arrive at the main message. If you worry that some audience members don't know as much about the topic as others, shift the background to pre-meetings, link to past papers and use the appendix. This avoids punishing those who are on top of the material and makes it easier for everyone to get to the heart of the matter. It will also help you cull unnecessary content.

I'll now walk through the three-parts of the introduction, offering visual clues like the one below to help you keep track of where we are up to in the overall structure.

This first navigator highlights the inverted triangle at the top of the structure, which refers to the introduction.

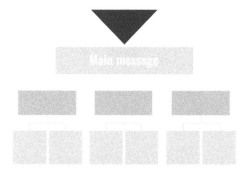

The introduction draws your audience toward your main message. Contrary to common practice, it is short – ideally no more than 15 per cent of the total document length. I begin by using a super simple camping example to explain how the three components of the introduction engage your audience in your topic.

Begin by explaining what you are discussing

If you have worked in consulting, you may have heard this first element described as 'the situation'.[1]

I prefer less jargon, and describe this element simply as 'what we are discussing'. It is typically a short sentence or two that lets your audience know which mutually relevant topic you are introducing.

It will most likely introduce a known problem or opportunity, or share an observation about a familiar situation. It should also be timely, topical and tight. Timely in that it covers recent information that should be familiar to the audience, topical in that it introduces the relevant topic for discussion and tight in that it is short!

This short section simply engages them in the issue. It helps them shift their mind from where it was to where you want it to be.

Make it relevant by explaining why you are discussing that topic now

Once your audience knows what you want to discuss, they will naturally want to know why that topic is relevant now. The diagram on the next page illustrates what happens inside our audience's heads as they read or listen to us speak.

I recommend using no more than two sentences to explain very simply why you are communicating with them now about the topic you have just introduced. It may be that you have a recommendation for them to consider, a request, an update or perhaps you need their help.

You may be able to make it more interesting than that, but it must point directly toward your main message.

Prime your audience to ask a question

Once your audience understands what you are discussing and why you are discussing it, they will naturally ask one, single obvious question that you can then answer with the main message.

This question might be something simple, such as 'What is your recommendation?', or perhaps, 'How should we proceed?'. Although this question rarely goes into your document, writing it on your message map focuses you on guiding your audience toward your main message. It also confirms for you the single, highest-order question you want to answer.

---

1   Although Barbara Minto recommends keeping this section really short, many consultants use this element differently. I commonly see the 'situation' become a lengthy description of the background rather than being used how it was originally intended.

Imagine, for example, if we were good friends and I said something like, 'The other day we talked about going away for a weekend'. You might then wonder, Why is my friend saying that? I would then naturally say, 'I have an idea', which would in turn lead you to wonder what my idea is.

Notice that in offering the thought 'I have an idea' I am not giving my answer away just yet, but I am priming my friend to be ready to hear what that idea, or main message, is.

This illustrates what can happen at the start of a paper or presentation. Explaining what you are discussing and why readies your audience for your main message, no matter how simple or complex the message, as below.

Distil your whole story into one single, insightful main message

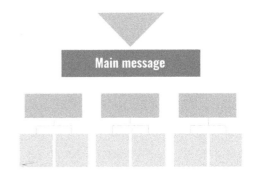

At 25 words or less, your main message is short, contains one single idea and packs a punch. It should be so relevant and powerful that your audience's response is 'Wow, that's useful', or 'Wow, that's insightful'.

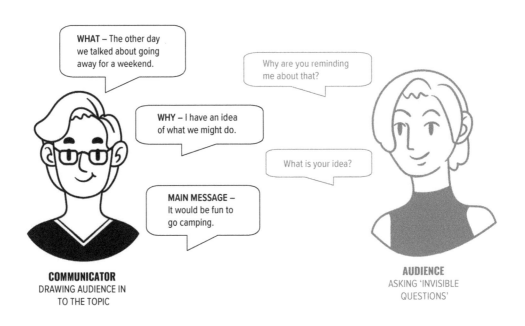

WHAT – The other day we talked about going away for a weekend.

Why are you reminding me about that?

WHY – I have an idea of what we might do.

What is your idea?

MAIN MESSAGE – It would be fun to go camping.

COMMUNICATOR
DRAWING AUDIENCE IN
TO THE TOPIC

AUDIENCE
ASKING 'INVISIBLE
QUESTIONS'

This main message is not a list of ideas strung together, but one single thought that captures the essence of the story.

It may summarise by describing what the data says, or synthesise to explain what the data means. Synthesis ties the facts to the situation, offering a clear point of view.

Offering this single, insightful message early in your communication will make your audience curious. The more insightful it is, the more curious they will be.

My value ladder below calibrates the difference between lower-value 'information' and more valuable ideas, or 'insights'. The difference is synthesis.

1. *Insight:* We recommend investing $2.4m next year to implement four stand-alone initiatives so we can meet our ambitious targets. *(Ideally this.)*
2. *Recommendation:* We recommend investing $2.4m to implement four stand-alone initiatives next year that will realign our IT and business strategies. *(Possibly this.)*
3. *Implication:* We identified six strategic themes that may impact our strategy. *(Possibly useful when updating your manager on your early stage findings.)*
4. *Information:* We identified six strategy themes. *(Unlikely this unless a junior researcher.)*

Not all messages deliver the same insight or VALUE ...

EXAMPLES

INSIGHT
Insights that resonate with leaders

We recommend investing $2.4m next year to implement four stand-alone initiatives so we can meet our ambitious targets.

RECOMMENDATION
Useful summary clearly expressed

We recommend investing $2.4m to implement four stand-alone initiatives next year that will realign our IT and business strategies.

IMPLICATION
Implication drawn from analysis

We identified six strategic themes that may impact our strategy.

INFORMATION
Useful observations about the facts

We identified six strategy themes.

Why is that relevant?

VALUE

Organise the ideas in a well-structured hierarchy

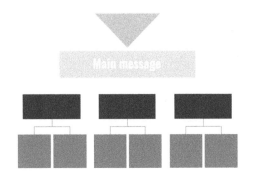

I use one of two frames to arrange supporting ideas. Both act like a 'thinking machine' that pushes you to think harder to articulate a clear and insightful point of view. They use logic and synthesis to help you clarify and convey your messaging so it is easy for your audience to grasp quickly.[2]

Here, I first share why I think these two ways of structuring your ideas suit business communication better than some others before explaining how they work.

Grouping and deductive structures come into their own for engaging busy leaders

I realise the idea of using just two structures might seem confining. It certainly did when I began using structured thinking in my early days at McKinsey. I had previously learned from authors and journalists who were all excellent communicators and wonderful teachers. They were experts in their genre.

When at teachers' college, I learned creative writing from Mem Fox, one of Australia's top children's authors, who shared wonderful techniques for writing creatively to entertain. (Her books, such as *Possum Magic* and *Wilfrid Gordon McDonald Partridge*, are magical.)

The creative writing techniques that Mem taught were, however, singly unsuited to untangling a 50-page finance deck, or to clarify and convey the top line of a complex narrative.

The journalism techniques I learned at university were also of limited help. These techniques were perfectly suited to writing news articles which called out a snappy headline. But they did not structure a message so that a time-poor audience could quickly find and unpick the logic behind the author's point of view. The headline idea was easy to find, but the reader must read to the end to find the underlying logic.

Other literary narrative structures suggest building the tension toward the big reveal. Holding your audience on that journey

---

2   William Minto first described using logic to communicate in *Logic: Inductive and Deductive*. Barbara Minto also discussed combining logic and synthesis to structure your messaging in *The Minto Pyramid Principle*.

requires great skill and, in my experience, creates great risk that you lose them on the way. The audience is also required to read to the end to find what they need, which senior audiences dislike.

I do want to assure you, however, that using grouping and deductive structures does not mean staying away from more sophisticated communication techniques altogether. You and your team can most certainly use them when necessary. You can add analogy and imagery when you need to entertain, perhaps when delivering a keynote speech.

For now, I will focus on helping you and your team crystallise messaging that will engage your decision-makers and drive the progress you need. Once you and your team have mastered this, feel free to become more creative and layer on sophisticated entertainment techniques.

Grouping and deductive structures are powerful thinking machines

I now offer a bird's-eye view of both grouping and deductive structures to help you see which structure has been used and, broadly, whether the structure is in good shape or not. As you can see, they look different and serve different purposes.

Grouping: Almost any type of message supported by individual ideas

Grouping structures are both tightly structured and enormously flexible, suiting almost any kind of communication. They support the main message with a list of two to five independent yet tightly connected ideas.

Deductive: Recommendation supported by chained reasons and an action

Deductive structures offer a powerful way to outline a recommendation when you must build the case for it and explain how to deliver it in the same communication. They offer three points, the first two outlining the reasons why your recommendation is strong before the final point explains how to implement it.

To put some meat on that, I'll first explain how grouping structures work, using a simple camping example. Then I will do the same for deductive structures before moving to more complex professional material.

Grouping structures consist of two to five points that support any kind of message

Groupings suit action plans, business cases, recommendations, requests, research findings, updates – anything.

The magic lies in five rules. These rules enable us to test that we have organised our ideas to offer a clear, compelling and cohesive point of view. Let me quickly outline them before exploring each one. Each idea must be:

- ▲ A single idea expressed as a full sentence.
- ▲ One of two to five ideas at that level.
- ▲ Closely related to the idea at the level above in the hierarchy.
- ▲ Ordered logically relative to its peers.
- ▲ Distinct and essential to conveying a cohesive point of view.

Each point must be a single idea expressed as a full sentence

This pushes you to clarify your thinking. Relying on dot points, words or phrases alone leads to unfinished thinking and sloppy communication. Let me illustrate.

Version 1 is a quick note:
Park Access Pass

Version 2 is a complete sentence:
Go online before Thursday to buy the Cougar Mountain Park Access Pass so we have permission to camp there.

The full sentence cannot be misconstrued and is easier to position within the message map. In contrast, the rough note is not complete, and so is easier to misconstrue and misplace.

Each point must be one of two to five at that level

I often hear people say you should have three points. While it's true that great speeches often anchor around three, it is not wise to force your thinking into three grouped ideas. This can force ideas into unnatural relationships, which in turn obscures or distorts the message.

Finding genuine and insightful connections between ideas is how we generate greater clarity and insight while also enabling us to sort ideas into a hierarchy. So, why these limits?

Two is the smallest number of ideas you can group. One idea on its own is not a group; it's just a single idea. When I see a single bullet point or a 'list of one' I ask myself whether that point is really a couple of ideas jammed into one or if it actually is a single idea.

If it really is a single idea, and there are no other obviously missing 'companion ideas', I merge it with the idea above.

Here's an example. The original section went as follows:

> *We need to book for our upcoming trip.*
>
> - *Camping site*

In this case I merged the two points into a single point like this:

> *We need to book a camping site for our upcoming trip.*

This is more cohesive and requires less brain strain from the reader.

More than five ideas indicates more thinking is needed. Sometimes you can get away with a list of six ideas, but it is rarely necessary. Long lists point to incomplete thinking. The connections between the ideas have not been sufficiently clarified.

To address this, look closely at the relationships between the ideas. Find what they have in common and group them.

The example in the column to the right has six dot points organised into three sections. The three mid-level messages add materially to the synthesis and resulting clarity, making the narrative easier to follow.

Each point must be closely related to the idea at the level above in the hierarchy

A concept I call the Power of One is the simplest way to understand this.

This concept is that *one* idea leads to *one* 'invisible' question from the audience, which leads to *one* type of response. This helps you clarify whether the ideas really do belong together and whether it looks like they do. So, I ask two sub-questions.

Firstly, do the ideas belong together?

By that I mean that if the idea primes your audience to ask 'Why is that true?', respond with reasons. For example, if I were to explain why camping would be the best getaway I could say something like this:

> *Main message: It would be fun to go camping at Cougar Mountain this weekend. Here's why:*
> 1. Cougar Mountain Park is great
>   - There is lots to do
>   - The area is beautiful and peaceful
> 2. You need a break
>   - You have been working too much
>   - You have time now your project is finished
> 3. I'll organise everything
>   - I have all the gear
>   - I know a great camping spot

This is persuasive in part because the ideas are relevant and well organised.

In contrast, mixing reasons, actions, criteria and facts is not only confusing, it is not persuasive.

In this next example you will see a confusing disconnect.

Main message: It would be fun to go camping this weekend.

1. Make the booking
   - Book accommodation
   - Book park pass
2. Camping is fun
   - You work too much
   - Reschedule your commitments
3. Prepare your gear
   - Check you have the gear you need
   - Pack your bag

This will frustrate my friend who likes camping and wants to know *how to make it happen.*

It is not clear whether you think the person you are speaking to likes camping or not. The first and third points are actions, explaining how to go camping. The middle point is a reason.

Identifying and fixing these disconnects clarifies the messaging, making it more useful for you and your audience. It is also much easier to find such errors when drawing the ideas into a hierarchy (as below) than when reviewing a fully drafted paper or presentation.

Secondly, are the ideas in each group expressed as though they match each other?

We can help our audience grasp our message more easily if we make it obvious that our ideas belong together.

I call using the same language pattern for each point in a list being 'parallel'. For example, these two ideas belong together but are not expressed as though they do:

- Gear is ready
- Pack your bag

Making them both actions, and parallel, increases clarity for you and your friend:

- Check your gear is ready
- Pack your bag

Being parallel is a terrific discipline because it helps flush out whether ideas really do belong together and then show the audience that they do.

Once you have clarified that the ideas not only belong together, but look like they do, you will want to decide how to order them within each group.

Each idea must be ordered logically relative to peers

I use two methods to organise grouped ideas within a communication: sequence and scale.

I most commonly sequence actions. This means placing actions in the order in which they need to be tackled. This might mean an audience member needs to take five steps to complete a task or perhaps to understand Part 1 before they can appreciate Part 2. It may also mean tackling the most important items first.

Scale is the simplest way to arrange ideas that are not ordered by time. To order ideas by scale, I identify the theme and then usually work from largest to smallest. This might mean offering my reluctant camping friend the most enticing idea first and working toward less enticing ideas.

In this case my theme is defined as what I think my friend will find enticing. Note that there may be a difference between what I find enticing and what they find enticing.

In other situations, I might begin with quick wins or small issues first to get them out of the way before introducing the major points.

The key is to use a deliberate order, which was lacking in the confused camping example to the left.

This helps further crystallise our insights while also making it easier for the audience to follow.

Each point must be distinct and essential to conveying a cohesive point of view

This is where experience and judgment are essential in evaluating the quality of thinking in a communication. Confirming that ideas are distinct and separate is typically not so difficult.

However, confirming that each idea is not only essential, but that the ideas together form a cohesive point of view can be phenomenally difficult.

Consultants use an acronym for this process which I will adopt here for the sake of potential familiarity and alignment.

That acronym is MECE, said Meee Seee. Some firms simplify it to NONG, which embodies some Australia humour which I love and will explain shortly.

I'll unpack it in three parts to help you use it effectively when thinking through your own messaging.

MECE stands for 'Mutually Exclusive, Collectively Exhaustive'

Before exploring the concept further, let me define it for you.

▲ *Mutually exclusive:* This test isn't so hard. It asks whether the ideas are distinct, i.e. separate, and don't overlap each other. Once you have ordered the ideas by sequence or scale, it should be fairly straightforward to resolve any gaps or overlaps, so long as each point is clearly articulated as a full sentence.

When I see clients use a phrase or a couple of key words my antenna goes up as this is where gaps and overlaps flourish.

▲ *Collectively exhaustive:* This one is harder. It asks you to assess whether the overall narrative is complete. Have you included all the ideas necessary to achieve your desired outcome?

There are two parts to this: one easier than the other.

First, have you included all of the ideas needed to support your main message? Have you covered all of the relevant issues required to support the main message as you have crafted it?

Secondly, double check whether this main message is actually sufficient. Have you posed the right question? For example, does your audience actually understand why your recommendation is solid and so only needs actions? Or, do they need to know why your recommendation matters? This can require quite a deal of judgement.

MECE allows topics to be discussed multiple times, so long as the message is distinct each time

In applying MECE, clients commonly confuse repeating topics with repeating ideas. By necessity, some topics, for example criteria for solving a problem, must be discussed multiple times within one communication.

The solution is to draft each point as a full sentence. This pushes you to say something about the criteria, not just to jot the name of the criteria down.

It is common, for example, to explain why one option is better than others. If so, you will describe how each option stacks up against each criterion. Each time you reference a criterion, you discuss it in relation to a different option.

In doing so you mention each criterion multiple times throughout the story, but in the context of a different idea.

I'll now come back to our camping example.

I'll lead with the main message and then offer two reasons that explain why one option is better than the other.

Each reason comments on the key decision-making criteria: cost, proximity to nature and comfort.

Main message: Camping would be a more fun and affordable way to soak in nature this weekend. Here's why:

1. Camping is less expensive and closer to nature than staying in an AirBNB, although admittedly less comfortable.
2. Staying at an AirBNB is more comfortable but also more expensive than camping and removes us from nature.

Each criterion is discussed against each option in a way that is relevant to that option.

MECE is a serious tool, yet can benefit from a bit of levity

Given MECE is used so widely in consulting, I am sticking with that. I do, however, like a simpler term: NONG. This stands for 'no overlaps, no gaps'. I like the irony of this. In Australian slang, 'nong' is short for 'ning nong', which is an insult used to describe a fool.

MECE – or NONG – is a deceptively simple test that can be very hard to get right. Those who master it are most definitely not fools.

Having now discussed how to group ideas, I'll offer a more detailed one-pager that pulls the key ideas together. I'll then move to deductive structures.

Visualising a grouping structure as a one-page message map

A short introduction that explains WHAT you are discussing. It should include information that is familiar to the audience and bring their minds to a recent relevant event or issue.	**One single insightful message that is 25 words or less and summarises or ideally synthesises your whole story.**		
	The single question your audience will naturally want to ask after learning your main message. This is unlikely to be written into your final document but helps power your thinking.		
Most likely a single sentence that explains WHY you want to discuss the topic outlined above with your audience now.	Point 1: The first of 2 to 5 points that respond to the same question your audience will naturally ask after hearing or reading the main message.	Point 2: The second of 2 to 5 points that responds to the same question the audience will naturally ask after hearing or reading the main message.	Points 3 to 5: More 'parallel' points if needed to further support the main message.
The question you want to answer, which your audience will naturally want to ask after they have heard or read what you are discussing and why.	• The first of 2 to 5 sub-points that form either a grouping or deductive structure to elaborate on the top-line point. • The second sub-point that follows the first, adopting either a grouping or deductive structure. • The third and subsequent sub-points, if necessary.	• As for point 1	• As for point 1

Deductive structures suit powerful recommendations

As for grouping structures, each point in a deductive chain needs to be a single, well-formed idea that synthesises or summarises the ideas below. The ideas are arranged differently, however.

In groupings, the two to five supporting points 'match' each other. In a deductive structure the three points are deliberately different. The first two set up the third.

Effective deductive structures follow three key rules. Each point:

1. has a specific role to play as a statement, comment or recommendation
2. must closely relate to the other two without overlapping
3. over arches a tightly knit grouping structure.

Let's unpack each of those further.

Each point has a specific role to play as a statement, comment or recommendation

The first two supporting points, the statement and comment, together persuade your audience why your recommendation is right. The idea is that by the time you have run through the first two sections your audience is persuaded and ready to hear how to implement your recommendation:

- ▲ The *statement* introduces an issue that is news to your audience and sets the broad parameters for the rest of your recommendation. You might call it your 'major statement' or your 'thesis' if you are harking back to any logic study that you have undertaken.
- ▲ The *comment* narrows the discussion to focus on one part of the statement. Some might call this a 'minor statement' or in some settings the 'anti-thesis'. It starts with 'However', or a similar connecting word.
- ▲ The *recommendation, or 'therefore'*, explains first what you recommend so you can then explain how to implement it. This is supported by your implementation plan.

Each point must closely relate to the other two without overlapping

The statement, comment and recommendation must be connected super tightly but not overlap. This is true when a deductive chain appears at the top line or lower down in the supporting structure.

I like to colour-code the points to test I have the flow right. You can see in the next camping example that I have one part of the statement and the matching part of the comment yellow, and then one part of the comment blue along with the corresponding part in the recommendation.

You can also see that each of the colour-coded ideas in the supporting points mirrors concepts in the main message.

Each point must over arch a tightly knit grouping structure

Mapping the ideas visually helps you focus on the relationships between the ideas.

You can see from the colour-coded example that each of the three top-line points sits above a grouped list. The same story in prose format looks like this:

Main message: Camping would be the most fun thing to do this weekend.

This high-level message ties all of the supporting points together.

Statement: We could do lots of things this weekend (a new idea that is broad and sits above evidence, as below)

- Watching movies would be easy
- Eating out would be social
- Camping would be relaxing

Comment: But, camping is the most fun thing to do (comments on the statement, which sits above evidence, expressed as reasons or evidence, as below)

- Camping is more fun than the other options
- We want to get out of town
- We can afford it

Recommendation: So, let's camp! (recommends the now obvious way forward before setting up the implementation plan, as below)
- Make the booking
- Change other plans
- Pack your gear

If you look closely at the supporting points for each of the three top-line points in the deductive chain, you can see that patterns again come into play.

The first two points are both supported by a mini Nugget pattern. Both points are supported by evidence. The third point, the recommendation, is supported by a Nike pattern, i.e. a list of actions.

Below I offer a more detailed one-pager so you can see clearly the relationships between the ideas in a deductive structure.

I hope this reinforces the value of visualising your ideas, too, rather than just jotting down a list of bullet points.

Visualising a deductive structure as a one-page message map

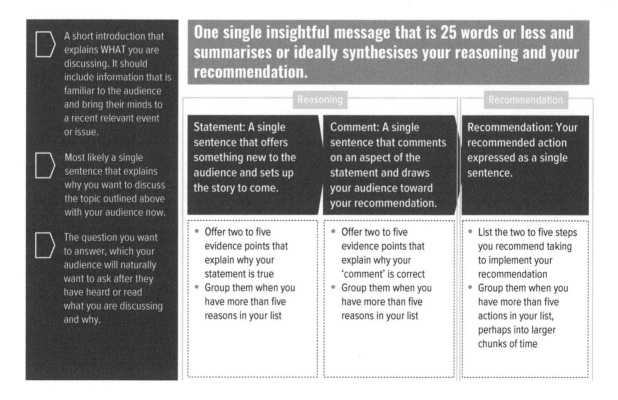

A short introduction that explains WHAT you are discussing. It should include information that is familiar to the audience and bring their minds to a recent relevant event or issue.

Most likely a single sentence that explains why you want to discuss the topic outlined above with your audience now.

The question you want to answer, which your audience will naturally want to ask after they have heard or read what you are discussing and why.

One single insightful message that is 25 words or less and summarises or ideally synthesises your reasoning and your recommendation.

Reasoning

Statement: A single sentence that offers something new to the audience and sets up the story to come.

Comment: A single sentence that comments on an aspect of the statement and draws your audience toward your recommendation.

Recommendation

Recommendation: Your recommended action expressed as a single sentence.

- Offer two to five evidence points that explain why your statement is true
- Group them when you have more than five reasons in your list

- Offer two to five evidence points that explain why your 'comment' is correct
- Group them when you have more than five reasons in your list

- List the two to five steps you recommend taking to implement your recommendation
- Group them when you have more than five actions in your list, perhaps into larger chunks of time

▲ SCORE the quality of your messaging

Now your ideas are sketched out as a message map, you want to test that they are strong. You want confidence that you are presenting a cohesive and compelling narrative that will help you deliver on your outcome.

This is where understanding the relationships between the ideas in your structure can help draw out the insights buried inside your own head and your team's heads also.

Over decades of being an outsider, I have learned that the structure itself can help find strengths and weaknesses in the messaging. It can lift you out of the detail to surface the insightful and impactful story you need to tell.

This has, in turn, led me by necessity to develop a fast technique for reviewing drafts.

I share my Scan, Score, Share technique with you here, so you can also benefit. I'll first explain how:

▲ Teaching lawyers turned my weakness into strength.

▲ Trusting the quality of the structure is a proxy for the quality of the thinking, and

▲ Working from the high-level messaging into the detail is fast and effective.

Teaching lawyers turned weakness into strength

In developing Scan, Score, Share, my weakness became my strength – and I hope it can for you too.

You might imagine my nerves when starting to teach lawyers how to write legal advice. Legal advice must be watertight. It's complicated, often convoluted and, regardless how well it's written, requires concentration to the very end. It is also rarely easy to read.

And lawyers are not only smart but also have a finely tuned appetite and ability for debate. This makes them good at their job. They would 'litigate' any suggestions I had – in part for fun and in part so they understood why and how they should tip their ideas about communication on their heads.

They were taught to first explain how they arrived at their insight. This was tricky as I recommend doing the opposite.

To top that, I needed to provide fast feedback on material I knew very little about to people who would quickly find fault.

How on earth? I relied on the only tool I had: structure.

Trusting the quality of the structure as a proxy for the quality of the thinking

I learned to trust that the structure, or shape, of the advice highlighted strengths and weaknesses in the quality of the thinking. This enabled me to find substantial problems within seconds without reading much, if anything, of the text. That might seem like a peculiar idea, so let me offer an analogy.

Imagine you are walking down the street to grab a coffee from your local café. As you stroll along you see the neighbour's dog. As usual, Fido has two ears, four legs and a tail. You barely notice the dog at all, unless of course you are friends and stop and give it a pat. You likely just think, *There goes Fido.*

If, however, one day you see that Fido is limping, you're likely to notice the limp more than anything else. Even if Fido were not familiar to you, you would notice the limp more than other features. The limp stands out in a way that the healthy dog does not. It might even make you sad as you wonder how it happened.

I realise your communication is more abstract and complex than Fido, but I want to illustrate the power of familiar shapes. For me, reviewing the legal advice became a bit like finding Fido's limp. The message map became 'healthy Fido', and the breaks in the structure a bit like a limp.

In scanning for structural misalignment, I would quickly see if everything was in good shape, or not. When I spotted misalignment, I could zero in to unpick what was happening at that point. This enabled me to provide fast feedback to my clients.

So, let's set you up to review your own communication quickly and, provide your team with fast feedback too.

Working from the high-level messaging into the detail is fast and effective

Working visually using a one-pager makes it easy to focus on the thinking that underpins communication and avoid getting lost in the details. You're not required to go on a time-consuming Easter egg hunt to find the insights.

The insights pop to the surface of the message map so you can scan and spot misalignment quickly – sometimes in seconds.

You can go through three steps to make that work. First, scan the message map to spot problems. Then, review more closely to score the communication against my SCORE framework. Finally, apply changes as needed or share your observations with the author.

I will now take you through these three steps one by one.

SCAN the message map to find thinking problems before reading (almost) anything

Now is a good time to remember Fido. Without wanting to over-stretch the analogy, imagine you have just seen Fido and without realising it you are checking to see if he's OK. Does he look happy? Well? Without any inkling that something might be wrong, you don't want to offer a full veterinary-grade checkup. You only want to take a quick look.

So, as with Fido, when reviewing the message map, start with the overall picture and then, after your preliminary view, you can dive deeper if you need to.

To explain how this works, I'll work from the general to the specific. I'll explain how I review the basic shape, section by section, before 'scoring' the communication during a deeper review.

So let's start our scan at beginning of the communication. Here's what I look for.

The introduction quickly draws your audience toward your main message

The introduction is short and includes three parts that together quickly draw your audience toward your main message. It does not provide screeds of background.

I look very quickly at the shape of these three introductory elements without reading them. Here's what I look for.

1. The *What* should be short. If it is bulging, you (or the author) has either explained new material or provided too much unnecessary background. Given an introduction should only contain timely material that should be known to the audience, this is a red flag. Elaboration is not needed, just a reminder.

2. The *Why* should be very, very short. If it is more than two sentences, you have a problem. The reason for communicating should be simple and short.

3. The *invisible audience question* should be so simple and obvious you think it's silly. The point of the 'what' and 'why' is to set up the audience to ask this question without even realising it. For now, just check that it looks short and simple.

The main message conveys the single most important idea in your communication

The main message should be one single sentence that is 25 words or less. If you have more than one sentence, you have a problem. If the box is bulging, you have a problem. If just a few words are in the box, you also have a problem. In all cases, synthesis is lacking.

Now is time to take a quick look at the shape of the supporting structure.

The structure backs up that message clearly and insightfully

The top-line structure sits right below the main message in our structure. It should include two to five top-line supporting points. If you only have one, or if you have more than five, you have a problem. If you have more than three points that include more than one starting with 'but' or 'however', you have a problem.

The supporting points should consist of two to five points in each list, with no more than one 'but' or 'however' in a deductive chain.

Using this framework, I can spot major structural problems in seconds. Although I typically register a few of the key words, I read almost nothing in this initial scan. If you trust the structure to work, you will be able to do so too.

Without even reading the words on the page, we have a crude sense of how well thought through the ideas are, and can spot some high-level areas for improvement.

SCORE the structure to diagnose substantive issues

Now we have an inkling as to whether Fido is in good shape, or whether he has a limp.

Let's diagnose what is going on. If limping, it's time to ask whether Fido hurt himself badly or simply has a minor sprain. And, although not wanting to think in the negative is tempting, doing so is the fastest way to find and fix substantive issues in your or your team's message map.

This is the hardest step for at least two reasons: it requires a decent understanding of message map 'mechanics', and it can be very tempting to fix each problem as soon as you find it. However, I urge caution. Stay out of the detail just yet, lean further into the structure and focus on correcting the thinking before rewriting.

I offer my SCORE framework now to help diagnose deeper strengths and weaknesses.

SCORE is scalable

Sometimes this summary of the SCORE framework will be sufficient to guide your review.

It asks if the one-pager provides quality content in a quality way by asking if it meets five key criteria. It asks whether it …

▲ **Sets** the scene quickly by drawing the audience toward one insightful message (Are the what, why and main message strong?).

▲ **Conveys** the right balance of strategic and operational detail (Are strategy and materiality appropriately catered for?).

▲ **Organises** the ideas in a well-structured hierarchy (Is the structure strong using grouping, deductive and MECE techniques?).

▲ **Readies** the audience quickly to achieve a quality outcome (Is it relevant and readable?).

▲ **Engages** the audience using a medium, style and tone that suits them (Is the communication skimmable and visual?).

You can download the summary below in the PowerPoint planner so you have it close by when reviewing your team's communication.

SCORE framework summary

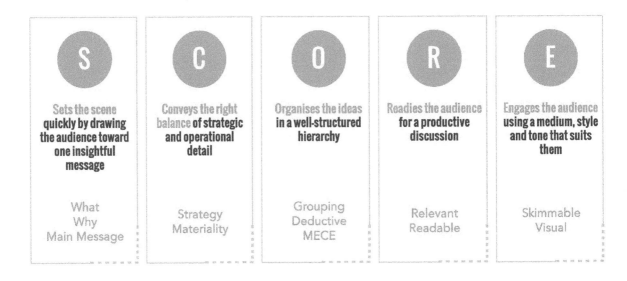

SCORE is comprehensive

Let's now 'double click' on each element. I imagine you will want to go more deeply into these for more significant communication so offer a complete list here for reference.

I ask whether the communication does the following. Does it ...

S – Set the scene quickly by drawing the audience toward one insightful message by ...

1. *Explaining* **WHAT** *is being discussed early:*
   a. Quickly reminding the audience about the familiar problem, opportunity or observation the paper will discuss
   b. Introducing that topic in a way that is timely and tight
2. *Explaining* **WHY** *this topic is being discussed now*
3. *Offering* **one insightful and visible main message** *that unifies the whole paper in 25 words or less*

C – Convey the right balance of strategic and operational detail by ...

4. *Positioning the story appropriately in relation to strategy*
5. *Aligning with the right materiality thresholds for this audience*

O – Organise the ideas in a well-structured hierarchy by ...

6. *Aligning ideas at every level of a grouping structure four ways:*
   a. Number: Each group has two to five ideas
   b. Type: Each idea is the same kind of idea as its peers
   c. Vertically: Each idea answers the single natural question prompted by the idea above
   d. Horizontally: Ideas are arranged logically, likely by sequence or scale
7. *Ensuring the top-line ideas in a deductive structure each play their specific role, i.e.:*
   a. The statement anchors the narrative around one substantive idea that is both new to the audience and broader in scope than the comment
   b. The comment narrows the discussion to focus on one key concept that was introduced in the statement
   c. The statement and comment are so persuasive that together they prepare your audience for your recommendation, so it does not come as a surprise

8. *Supporting the top-line of a deductive structure well, which means that:*

    a. Both the statement and comment are supported by tightly grouped ideas

    b. The recommendation ('therefore') is supported by tightly grouped actions

9. Avoiding gaps and overlaps, *i.e.* the ideas are MECE (Mutually Exclusive, Collectively Exhaustive). This involves:

    - Categorising and labeling ideas correctly

    - Avoiding ideas overlapping each other

    - Leaving nothing out

R – Ready the audience for a productive discussion by ...

10. *Focusing only on matters relevant to the desired outcome*

11. *Being easily readable, using language that is active and parallel throughout, i.e. by:*

    a. Synthesising or summarising ideas at every level into fully formed sentences that the audience will find insightful, i.e. they are useful, impactful and interesting

    b. Expressing ideas clearly, so the audience doesn't need to ask for clarification

    c. Using parallel language so the ideas obviously match each other

E – Engage the audience using a medium, style and tone that suits them by ...

12. *Formatting ideas so it is easy to skim the hierarchy of the messaging, in any medium*

13. *Using simple images, charts and diagrams to help the audience quickly grasp ideas*

Make sure you download the summary along with the associated scoring rubric before your one-month free Clarity Hub[1] access expires if you have not yet done so.

Before practising this process on an example, I'll give you some ideas for sharing your observations with your team.

SHARE your insights in the most suitable way

Here are some thoughts to help iterate the messaging before preparing the final document:

▲ Share the SCORE framework with your team before you ask them to prepare a draft. This way they will know what you are using to review their messaging.

▲ Begin by calling out the strengths in the draft. This will reinforce what is working while also create a tone that allows for suggestions. Even in quite poor examples, there are still a few positives

---

1   ClarityFirstProgram.com/ClarityHub

to observe. At a minimum, you might note that they 'had a go' at using the techniques, or that the key ideas are included even if they need significant tightening or reorganising.

▲ Use the language of structure to explain what you want changed. This means, for example, correctly labeling the 'what', the 'why', main message and the top line structure. If using a deductive chain, then name each element accurately as a statement, comment and recommendation. This helps everyone discuss their structures and get above the detail when working with you and with each other.

▲ Annotate why you have recommended changes. You may use the comments function to do this or add coloured text onto the PowerPoint slide, e.g. if ...

- ideas are not parallel, you might say, 'I have tweaked the format of these sentences so the ideas belong together. It is then easier to see if the section is complete'.

- ideas are not well synthesised, you might say, 'I elevated the synthesis to draw out the message for each point'.

- ideas are missing, you might say, 'I added two extra points so we deliver a comprehensive case'.

- deductive chains are not well linked, you might say, 'I have more tightly connected the three top-line points so the reader is fully persuaded before they get to the recommendation'.

Now it's time to see how an example evolves so you can see the difference between strong and weak.

▲ Review an example to see the difference between strong and weak

I love helping clients see what is possible. When working with professionals of mixed communication ability, it can be hard to know what good really looks like.

To help with that I will give you the opportunity to review an IT strategy example as we iterate it from 'just OK' to much, much better.

I'll first introduce the situation around that paper before working through each step in the Scan, Score and Share journey with you.

Step 1: Understand the context. The executive needed Board approval for their new IT strategy

In this situation, an industry body needed to better align their IT strategy with their business strategy.

The IT environment in their organisation was relatively simple and not terribly mature.

The relationship between the executive and the Board was cordial and familiar, given the organisation was small and the team was high-performing.

This is good news in reviewing this draft, as we can put stakeholder complexities to the side and focus on the messaging alone.

Step 2: Scan, don't read, the draft

I encourage you to scan the structure on the facing page, keeping in mind the high-level structuring principles I covered in the last chapter. Here's a quick recap:

- Focus first on the big-picture structure. Remember Fido? We are looking to see whether he is structurally sound first, using that as clues to find deeper problems. This means looking at the size of sections and the number of items in each.
- Avoid reading anything more than the occasional word just yet.
- Note down your high-level observations for the sake of this exercise to reinforce what you are doing here now.
- Remember this should take seconds.

Even if it seems odd, resist the temptation to read deeply just yet. Just scan it, record the ideas as they occur to you, and then review my notes. We will go deep shortly.

Exercise:

Company X wanted to review the IT environment from a business lens and assess fit for purpose.

Cloud and IT strategy existed, but it was not developed in response to the business strategic priorities.

What is the best IT strategy for Company X moving forward to ensure we enable our strategic objectives and delivery?

Scan this draft

Answer: Six strategy themes were identified that will deliver and align with IT Strategy. Four viable initiatives were identified for the coming FY with an implementation will cost of $2.4m; however, each is independent in its delivery.

Initiative 1: Foundational enhancements to stakeholder and third-party interactions	Initiative 2: Migrate office productivity & collaboration tools, Tool 1 and Tool 2 from Treasury-hosted environment to Microsoft Cloud	Initiative 3: Digital Records Management	Initiative 4: Secure response and recoverable foundations
Outcome: Enhanced stakeholder and third-party interactions.	**Outcome:** • 20% reduction in annual IT operating costs • Improved productivity through reduced complexity for users • Enhanced office collaboration & productivity tools	**Outcome:** Enhanced stakeholder and third-party interactions	**Outcome:** Improved information security and business recoverability
Cost: XXXXX	**Cost:** XXXX	**Cost:** XXXX	**Cost:** XXXX
High-level activities: • Foundational single view of customer in CRM • Redesign website • Social publishing (LinkedIn)	**High-level activities:** • Migration of existing applications & tools office productivity & collaborations & associated data • Develop Multisite backup & DR • Develop third-party support & maintenance • Promote new ways of working using new collaboration tools	**High-level activities:** • Define current data and records • Develop SharePoint libraries to store digitised records • Scan and upload paper records	**High-level activities:** • Horizon 1: Half yearly cyber security review & IT security risk reviewed by internal audit • Horizon 2: Half-yearly DR tests & multisite disaster recovery for business applications

Step 3: Compare our notes

As with most structures, some things work in this draft, while others don't.

Several aspects of the structure work well

1. The 'what', 'why' and 'question' are about the right length. They are not 'bulging' with background, nor are they just a couple of words.
2. Each of the four supporting points starts with a category, which tells me they are 'the same kind of thing' or, as I call it, conceptually aligned or 'parallel'.
3. A healthy number of supporting points has been included at the top line and also within each section underneath.

Some other aspects require attention

1. The main message box is bulging with too many words.
2. The main message box has two sentences, when it should have only one.
3. The ideas supporting each initiative are chunked by category. I can see this because they are single, bolded words. This shows that the ideas are not fully formed as messages.

So, without even reading the words on the page, we can spot some areas for improvement.

Given the shape has problems, we need to diagnose further to better understand the nature of those problems.

Step 4: SCORE to identify deeper issues

Before reading this section, go back to the deeper SCORE questions and conduct your own review. You may like to flip between that page and the one-pager, or perhaps photocopy the SCORE questions to avoid page flipping. Then come back and compare against my review. Here are my notes.

S - Sets the scene - The introduction and main message do not set the right scene quickly

On the next page I share my notes on the introduction. I revisit the questions I use to assess whether an introduction sets the audience up well as I review the IT strategy example.

As you will see, all the information is there – but the audience has to work too hard to find the message.

This is one of the most common challenges I see and it occurs because the author's thinking wasn't complete.

The IT strategy introduction is off topic, leading to a rambling main message

Scene-setting questions	Comments
Does the draft provide context by explaining WHAT topic is being discussed early? This might be a known problem, opportunity or observation that will be the focus for the paper. Here's the original text: Company X wanted to review the IT environment from a business lens and assess fit for purpose.	It is too general. Doesn't drill into the actual issue at hand: the disconnect between the cloud and IT strategies and the business's strategic priorities.
Does it introduce the topic in a way that is timely?	No. This describes the purpose of the review that was established some time ago. It is not timely.
Does it quickly remind the audience of what they should already know? May reference and/or link to past papers. No longer than 15% of the total document.	No. It quickly reminds the audience about the wrong issue. They do know that they wanted to review the IT environment from a business lens and assess its fit, but it's not the right topic for this paper.
Does it explain WHY this topic is being discussed with this audience now – i.e. what triggered this communication? Here's the original text: A cloud and IT strategy existed, but it was not developed in response to the business strategic priorities.	It doesn't explain why the topic is being discussed now but rather describes the problem being solved. This information better describes what we are communicating about, and so belongs in the 'what' section above the 'why' in the message map. This is a common challenge as people try to articulate why they are really communicating with this audience right now about the topic they have just introduced.
Does it offer one insightful main message? This single, insightful main message should be visible at first glance and unify the whole paper in 25 words or less. Here's the original text: Six strategy themes were identified that will deliver and align with IT Strategy. Four viable initiatives were identified for the coming FY with an implementation cost of $2.4m; however, each is independent in its delivery.	The main message is too long at 35 words and split over two sentences. It also lacks insight.

C - Conveys the right balance of strategic and operational detail - The example is sound regarding strategy and materiality

This element relies on judgment as well as specific structural tests. Each stakeholder group has different preferences, and these are not static. As their situations change, so can their preferences. I'll expand what I look for before sharing what I saw.

What I look for in general

Firstly, does the author position the narrative within the strategy? This might be the organisational strategy or the one for your specific team, or both. In being useful, the communication needs to help the organisation make progress. Aligning to the strategy is a useful and critical test.

Secondly, does the narrative align with the appropriate materiality thresholds? You may want to refer to the formal materiality thresholds outlined in your organisation's governance framework. If your immediate colleagues or manager aren't sure, you can go to others in your organisation for help. Your company secretary will be able to help you with this if you are engaging your board and senior leaders, or perhaps your CEO's assistant can help for the senior leadership team. It may also help to review past papers and comments from participants in analogous meetings.

What I saw in the IT strategy example

While the information in this story isn't yet well formed, it does position itself well within the strategy and align to materiality thresholds.

O - Organises the ideas in a well-structured hierarchy - Both sample grouping and deductive structures lack synthesis, even though they are MECE

I want to be comprehensive here in illustrating the approach, so will work through this structural review in three parts.

I'll begin reviewing the grouping structure I initially shared with you.

I then offer a poor deductive structure to give you an opportunity to review that structural type. This also highlights that many stories can be shared many ways.

Lastly, I will ask whether the grouping structure is MECE, i.e. whether the ideas are mutually exclusive and collectively exhaustive. This test is also relevant to deductive structures, but one example review is sufficient.

On the next page, I explain why I think the initial grouping structure is weak. Although the points are obviously grouped, the quality of that grouping is not strong as it lacks synthesis.

The grouping structure lacks synthesis

Grouping questions	Comments
Number: Does each group have two to five ideas? Here is the original text for reference: Initiative 1: Foundational enhancements to stakeholder and third-party interactions Initiative 2: Migrate office productivity & collaboration tools, Tool 1 and Tool 2 from Treasury-hosted environment to Microsoft Cloud Initiative 3: Digital Records Management Initiative 4: Secure response and recoverable foundations	Sort of. There are two to five points in each section, both at the top-line level (in the coloured boxes directly under the main message) and in the supporting levels. However, they are not ideas. One of the supporting ideas, under the third point, is a repeat of the idea under the first point though. This is likely a 'copy-paste error' that needs fixing.
Type: Is each idea the same kind of idea as its peers?	These are nearly all the same type, but are not always 'ideas'. Top-line – these are all labeled 'initiatives', which is an encouraging start. The language used to describe each one is not consistent, though, which makes me ask whether each idea really is an 'initiative'. For example, digital records management is a label or a category, not an initiative. Supporting points – these have been 'bucketed' into topics rather than distilled into messages, which means it is 'insight light'. The 'buckets' collect ideas that relate to the topic rather than to the message. Although in this case these points are in the right section of the story, 'dumping' them rather than synthesising them leaves the audience to tie the messaging together, rather than the author doing their job.
Vertical relationships: Does each idea answer the single natural question prompted by the idea above?	No. The ideas are a random assortment of things 'thrown' into 'buckets' rather than tied together to form messages within a cohesive story. This requires the audience to do too much work and leaves the author exposed to the risk that the audience will misunderstand them, or not read the detail as it is too complicated.
Horizontal order: Are the ideas arranged using a logical order – likely sequence or scale?	Mostly, yes. The top line is ordered by scale, with the most important initiative listed first. The lower levels are mostly well ordered also.

Let's now see how it might look if we used a deductive structure. You will see that I have reused the what, why and question, but have offered a weak main message above an equally weak deductive chain.

You may like to review it against my key evaluation questions. At this stage, just look at the top line. By this I mean the three points that sit right below the main message. Ask yourself these questions:

- Does the main message link with the supporting messaging?
- Do the top-line points form a cohesive deductive structure that leads to one powerful recommendation?
- Are the points that support the top-line chain well grouped?

Review to see what you think and then compare with my notes to the right.

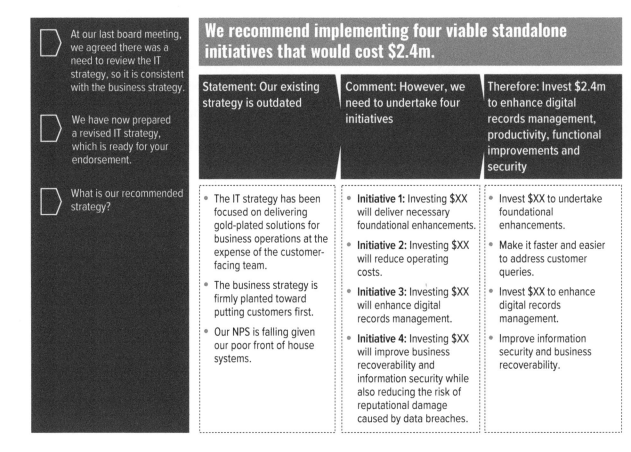

At our last board meeting, we agreed there was a need to review the IT strategy, so it is consistent with the business strategy.

We have now prepared a revised IT strategy, which is ready for your endorsement.

What is our recommended strategy?

We recommend implementing four viable standalone initiatives that would cost $2.4m.

Statement: Our existing strategy is outdated	Comment: However, we need to undertake four initiatives	Therefore: Invest $2.4m to enhance digital records management, productivity, functional improvements and security
• The IT strategy has been focused on delivering gold-plated solutions for business operations at the expense of the customer-facing team. • The business strategy is firmly planted toward putting customers first. • Our NPS is falling given our poor front of house systems.	• **Initiative 1:** Investing $XX will deliver necessary foundational enhancements. • **Initiative 2:** Investing $XX will reduce operating costs. • **Initiative 3:** Investing $XX will enhance digital records management. • **Initiative 4:** Investing $XX will improve business recoverability and information security while also reducing the risk of reputational damage caused by data breaches.	• Invest $XX to undertake foundational enhancements. • Make it faster and easier to address customer queries. • Invest $XX to enhance digital records management. • Improve information security and business recoverability.

This deductive version also lacked synthesis

Questions for the top line	Comments
Does the statement anchor the narrative around one substantive idea that is both new to the audience and broader in scope than the comment? Here is the original text for reference: *Our existing strategy is outdated*	The statement is broad but so generic that it is hard to evaluate. It is not insightful and is unlikely to be news to decision-makers.
Does the comment focus on one key concept that was introduced in the statement? *However, we need to undertake four initiatives*	Does not link to the statement. This is a separate idea that is related but not intrinsically linked to the same topic. It is also intellectually blank. All it says is that there are four initiatives; it lacks substance and insight.
Is it reasonable to expect that the audience is persuaded in your recommendation by the time they have read the statement and comment, or does it come as a surprise? *Therefore, invest $2.4m to enhance digital records management, productivity, functional improvements and security*	No. This appears out of nowhere! The audience is not prepared for the idea that they should invest $2.4 million by reading the top line only. It is also a list of ideas that belongs in the level below rather than a single and insightful point that glues those supporting ideas together.

Questions for the second line	Comments
Are both the statement and comment supported by tightly grouped reasons?	No. The statement is supported by a mix of reasons and statements of fact. For example, 'the business strategy is firmly planted toward putting customers first' is an observation that does not do anything other than describe the existing situation. It is also unlikely to be news. The supporting points under the comment do *try* to explain why spending a certain amount of money will deliver a benefit, but they are weakly expressed. They lack substance.
Is the 'therefore' recommendation supported by tightly grouped actions?	These points are actions, but they are too general to be useful. They do not demonstrate that the author has thought about the actions that need to be undertaken to improve the IT strategy. They are also in mixed format, with the ideas not being parallel. Some include a financial element, but others do not, leaving me wondering if they are free!

Although poorly expressed, the ideas in the grouping are MECE

Although I think the ideas in the original grouping are expressed poorly, they are MECE. They are well categorised and labeled, separate and complete.

Now that you have a view about the integrity of the structure, you need to ask yourself whether it is fit for purpose. It needs to both 'tell the answer' and 'tell the story'.

By this I mean it goes further than explaining what is technically accurate to explaining how this 'answer' can help drive progress.

R - Readies the audience for a productive discussion - I give the grouping half marks

This again requires judgement combined with a good understanding of your stakeholders and their needs.

When I think about readying the audience for a productive discussion, I want them to not only read the communication quickly and easily, but understand it without wasting time. This means they won't take up time in the meeting clarifying the ideas in the paper and potentially delaying or not taking the action you need.

This doesn't assume automatic approval, but that stakeholders will be able to quickly evaluate and discuss it intelligently. See my responses below.

Readiness questions	Comments
Does the message map focus only on matters relevant to the desired outcome?	Yes.
Are the ideas synthesised and summarised at every level into fully formed sentences that *the audience will find insightful?*	No. Many of the points were not ideas, which by definition means they are not fully formed sentences and cannot be insightful.
Are the ideas expressed clearly with little need for clarification?	No. The 'voice over' in the subsequent meeting was needed to cover up for the weaknesses in the individual points and to string them together. The messaging did not stand alone.

E - Engages the audience - This message map only weakly engages the audience

Some organisations use templates to tightly prescribe the way information is presented to senior leaders, while others offer a great degree of freedom.

The key is to understand the requirements of your specific senior stakeholder group and to accommodate those. If unsure, err on the side of formality and respect while avoiding being boring and stiff.

The table below outlines key things to look for, again commenting on the IT strategy grouping. These are again relatively straightforward ideas that require little introduction.

At the one-page stage, ask yourself whether the way your or your team's points are drafted will translate well into the final paper or presentation form.

I do note also that I am providing comments here on a one-pager, rather than a full document. These engagement questions are better suited to the final paper or presentation. I do hope, however, that this quick illustration makes the point.

To drive that home, on the next page I rework the IT strategy grouping to show you how much stronger it could have been.

Engagement questions	Comments
Is the messaging easy to skim, regardless of the chosen medium?	The messages were buried inside 'topics' or 'buckets'. This makes them hard to find, slowing down the audience and requiring them to do a lot of the thinking work themselves.
Have images, charts and diagrams been used wherever possible to help the audience quickly grasp the ideas?	This is only relevant when reviewing a paper or presentation. I will, however, call out one important point. I see clients reworking the message map to remove the main message and sometimes also the top line points. Changing this visual format does not help the author synthesise their points, nor the audience grasp them.

This stronger grouping structure suits an audience that needs little persuasion

At our last board meeting, we agreed to review the IT strategy to better align it with the business strategy.

Our revised IT strategy, is now ready for your endorsement.

What is your strategy?

We recommend investing $2.4m in 2024 to implement four viable, standalone initiatives to align our IT and business strategies and support efficiency and growth.

Initiative 1: Invest $XX to improve our foundational systems supporting customer and stake-holder experience.	**Initiative 2:** Invest $XX to upgrade productivity and collaboration tools to reduce operating costs.	**Initiative 3:** Invest $XX to enhance Digital Records Management.	**Initiative 3:** Invest $XX to improve information security and business recoverability.
• Create foundational single view of customers in the Customer Relation-ship Management system. • Redesign website. • Improve social publishing (LinkedIn).	• Migrate existing applications, office productivity and collaboration tools and associated data from the on-prem servers to Microsoft Cloud. • Develop multi-site backup and disaster recovery. • Enter into third-party support and maintenance agreements. • Promote new ways of working using new tools.	• Define current data and records. • Develop SharePoint libraries to store digitised records. • Scan and upload paper records.	• **Horizon 1:** Undertake half-yearly cyber security review and IT security risk audit, which will be reviewed by internal audit. • **Horizon 2:** Undertake half-yearly disaster recovery tests and multi-site disaster recovery for business applications.

This stronger deductive version would suit an audience that needs more persuasion than the grouping offers

At our last board meeting, we agreed to review the IT strategy to better align it with the business strategy.

Our revised IT strategy, is now ready for your endorsement.

What is your strategy?

We recommend investing $2.4m in 2024 to implement four viable, standalone initiatives to align our IT and business strategies and support efficiency and growth.

Four ingredients are central to better aligning our IT and business strategies.	Investing $2.4m to implement four key initiatives will create the necessary IT and business alignment.	Therefore, allocate $2.4m to implement four key initiatives during 2024
• The IT strategy needs to prioritise customers rather than gold-plated business operations. • The IT strategy needs to support productivity and collaboration. • The IT strategy needs to support faster answers to customer questions. • The IT strategy needs to underwrite business recoverability and data security.	• **Initiative 1:** Investing $XX will deliver necessary foundational enhancements to improve stakeholder and customer experience. • **Initiative 2:** Investing $XX to upgrade productivity and collaboration tools will reduce opex costs. • **Initiative 3:** Investing $XX will enhance digital records management, making it faster and easier to answer customer queries. • **Initiative 4:** Investing $XX will improve business recoverability and information security while also reducing the risk of reputational damage caused by data breaches.	• Endorse program approach and $2.4m budget. • Stand up a project team to drive the program mid January 2024. • Schedule foundational work to be complete by end of April. • Progress the remaining initiatives in parallel, aiming for November compeltion. • Report monthly on progress.

▲ Structure the messaging for a communication of your own

You may be tempted to keep reading and learn more, but you may do better to pause and try the ideas out. How many great books have you enjoyed, and then never implemented the author's ideas?

Perhaps you are familiar with this maxim?

I hear and I forget
I see and I remember
I do and I understand

So, now is the time. Stop reading and start doing so that the ideas sink in.

As just mentioned, I recommend working through the process with a small piece of communication to make it both practical and easy. Here are five steps to take:

1. Think of a modest piece of communication you need to prepare. This could be a paper that feels pretty straightforward, an email you need to think through (that is, one that's more than 10 lines long and requires some thought), or perhaps even a message you want to convey verbally in an upcoming meeting.

2. Download the PowerPoint Planner from the Clarity Hub Toolkit[1].

3. Start working through the planner process, even if it feels like overkill for your sample communication by

   a. dumping down your initial thoughts on the brainstorm page to gather your thoughts

   b. flushing out your strategy to clarify your desired outcome (don't skip this bit!)

   c. firming up your message, beginning with the idea that is clearest and working around it.

4. Reviewing against the SCORE framework, double clicking on each area for thoroughness, to check you have 'nailed' the messaging.

5. Flipping it into the right document format, whether that is an email, paper or presentation.

You will be better placed to lead your team if you use the ideas yourself than if you just read about them. The next chapter will also have more meaning if you have 'had a go' rather than just kept reading.

---

1   ClarityFirstProgram.com/ClarityHub

CHAPTER 5

Settle the document to maintain the integrity of the messaging

Now your thinking is clear and the team has finalised their one-pager, they will translate it into a document. Your next step is to review the document to gain confidence that it matches your needs and expectations. Ideally, this will involve a quick Scan, Score, Share process where you again lean on the structure of the messaging to evaluate the quality of the material.

I recommend tightly linking the hierarchy of your messaging with the formatting of your document – whether it is an email, a paper or a presentation. To do this, you need to do five things:

1. Understand the connection between message maps and documents.
2. Connect the dots using the 105 reports example.
3. Factor in prescriptive corporate templates where needed.
4. Know how to quickly review papers and presentations.
5. Present with polish.

▲ Understand the connection between message maps and documents

Having invested in preparing a tightly structured and insightful message map, now is not the time for your team to bury the insights.

To that end, I recommend maintaining a strong connection between your message map and your document. This ensures ideas are easy to find. Here are the three steps to take:

1. Tailor the title to convey the right tone.
2. Begin with a well-structured executive summary.
3. Visualise the messaging so the audience can easily skim the headlines.

Tailor the title to convey the right tone

I differentiate my approach for the title to suit the sensitivity of the messaging.

When a message is sensitive or perhaps unusually controversial, it pays to hold it back until you can introduce it properly. In these instances, I recommend using the title to describe what you are discussing. Said another way, I use the type of meeting as the title. For example, for the 105 reports example you might say 'Legacy Reports Project Update'.

If the main message is not so sensitive or is just plain good news, then tighten it to become akin to a newspaper headline. For example, you might say 'Legacy Reports Project on track across all key areas'. This approach would be risky for this example, which involves a delicate message. Beginning with a title that says something like, 'Need to decide whether to spend

more or renegotiate with the regulator for Report Project' would also be provocative. In situations like these, you might choose a different path.

Alternatively, you might want to draw stakeholder attention to the importance of the current juncture without giving the game away. You might say something like, 'Critical decision point for Legacy Reports Project'. You could even nudge the urgency further by saying something like 'Critical decision needed to determine direction for Legacy Reports Project'.

Your title choice is determined by your judgement as to what will be most effective in your current situation.

Once that is established, you can move to the executive summary.

I have outlined options for easy reference below.

Type	Options for titles
Meeting type	Legacy Reports Project Update
Main message	Need to decide whether to spend more or negotiate with regulator
Discussion topic	Critical decision point for Legacy Reports Project
The ask	Critical decision needed to determine direction for Legacy Reports Project

Begin with a well-structured executive summary

If your document is longer than half a page, you need an executive summary. Regardless of the format, this will include your introduction, main message and top-line points.

Here a few thoughts to help you prepare yours.

1. Adjust the order of the items in the introduction to suit your tone. Using the 'classic order' I introduced earlier ('What', 'Why' and then main message) is clear and straightforward, but slightly softer than some other options. In contrast, beginning with the main message or 'why' strengthens the tone. If you experiment with this for an example of your own, you will see what I mean. Emails are the perfect playground as you will quickly see the tonal shifts.

2. Next, offer the top-line points as a list, or even better, use a diagram to visualise the concepts you are discussing.
   The easiest way to find a suitable framework or diagram is to use an image library. Many organisations have them, and my colleague Neil Young offers such a library with 300 high-quality visuals inside. You can download a sample inside the Clarity Hub, or purchase the whole 300 on my site[1].

3. Expand the executive summary if needed. If you and your team are preparing a lengthy paper, you may include a short paragraph for each point in the executive summary. Most business communication, however, only needs the top-line points.

Visualise the messaging so the audience can easily skim the headlines

I encourage you to use visual cues to differentiate the value of each point. The bigger the idea, the more visible it should be so the audience can grasp it immediately.

If you skim this book, you will see this technique in play. If your formatting matches the hierarchy of your messaging, your audience will be able to quickly find what they need. This is especially important for business communication. Your audience is not sitting on a beach relaxing into a novel. They are working against the clock to add value. Your communication needs to help them do that.

---

1   ClarityFirstProgram.com/ImageLibrary

▲ Connect the dots using the 105 reports example

The coming pages showcase how the 105 reports message map operates in both presentation and paper format. Translating the message map structure into document format is relatively straightforward, so I will illustrate more than explain using an annotated example.

Before I go there, however, I will call out some practicalities for each format.

Practicalities for presentations

I have kept this presentation fairly high level on the assumption that the steering committee was familiar with the issues and could refer to detailed financial breakdowns in the appendix.

This makes it easy to see the links between the message map and the document.

Should you want some more complex examples, check out my PowerPoint Toolkit, which illustrates how some very different structures play out in PowerPoint. At the time of writing, I offer seven sanitised real-world professional examples, but plan to add more.[2]

Practicalities for papers

The 105 reports example needs to be presented to a senior decision-making body which uses a template. Here are my thoughts about how I link simple templates with a message map:

▲ The 'Recommendation' section usually includes the main message, explaining what you are asking the decision-making group to sign off against. In this case, the recommendation is more general so I handled it differently.

▲ The 'Executive summary' provides a complete high-level overview of the story, structured to match the message map itself.

▲ The 'Discussion' unpacks each of the supporting points from the high-level story, offering more detail on each.

▲ The 'Attachments' section caters for the extra detail a manager might require to be confident in the substance. Members of this leadership group may also want to review the financials, but some will trust the managers to have reviewed these thoroughly, rendering the attachments section the most appropriate place for these details.

---

2 ClarityFirstProgram.com/Decks

This 105 Reports message map sets up the storyboard, the PowerPoint deck and the Board Paper

Meeting regulatory requirements requires us to transition all 105 legacy reports into the case system by the end of this financial year. We have now reviewed the associated work plans and received updated estimates.

We are now ready to share those estimates with you along with potential ways forward.

What are you suggesting?

Delivering the 105 reports means either investing $1.2m to $2m more over the coming two years or renegotiating requirements with the regulator.

Despite stress testing all budgets, we can't transition all 105 regulatory reports within the agreed $2m budget this financial year.	This means we need to make trade-offs when finalising the project workplans.	Therefore, we ask you to advise which tradeoffs we can make.
Updated estimates for database came back at $2m, which is 2.5 x the original budget due to more comprehensive scoping. **Budgets for other aspects of the work have not materially changed.** • Workflow remains same. • API linking ditto. • Operational teams ditto. **Work required for reports identified since June last year has not been factored in.**	**We could meet the scope by spending $1.2m to $2m more over the coming two years.** • We could deliver everything in FY23 with $1.2m more during FY23, or • We could deliver some in FY23, some in FY24 with $2m or more in total. **We could renegotiate scope or time with the regulator.** • We could limit the scope and deliver only the top 70 reports by FY23 (fix existing 36, do another 35ish) within the current budget, or • We could seek agreement from the regulator to further extend the project and deliver all at a later date.	**Decide whether to spend more ...** • Decide whether to increase funding by $1.2m for FY23. • Decide whether to budget $2m more for the project in total and roll into next year. **Decide whether to renegotiate ...** • Decide whether to pitch the regulator to accept the top 70 reports as adequate for FY23. • Decide whether to seek extensions.

Title page explains why we are presenting re: the legacy reports

Background page offers the what and why (hide when presenting)

Meeting regulatory requirements requires us to transition all 105 legacy reports into the case system by the end of this financial year.

We have now reviewed plans and estimates and are ready to discuss potential ways forward.

Executive summary offers high level message + navigation aid

We need to decide to either spend $1.2 million to $2 million more over the coming two years or to renegotiate requirements with the regulator

Navigator in top right corner of each page

Despite stress-testing all budgets, we can't transition all 105 regulatory reports within the agreed $2 million budget this financial year

 01 — Updated estimates for database came back at $2m, which is 2.5 x the original budget due to more comprehensive scoping. (See appendix for breakdown.)

 02 — Budgets for other aspects of the work have not materially changed. Costs for workflow, API linking, and operational aspects remain steady.

 03 — Work required for reports identified since June last year has not been factored in.

Title of each page is the message

This means we need to make trade-offs when rescoping the project workplans

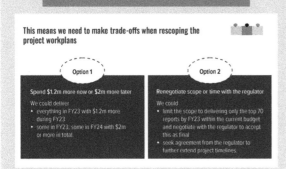

Repetitive wording removed and language tightened

We ask you to advise which trade-offs we can make

We need to decide whether we

Spend more by
1. increasing funding by $1.2m for FY23
2. budgeting $2m more for the project in total and roll into next year.

Renegotiate by
1. accepting the top 70 reports in FY23 as adequate and convincing the regulator to agree
2. seeking extensions from the regulator.

LEGACY REPORT PROGRAM – CRITICAL DECISION POINT RE: PATH FORWARD FOR 105 REPORTS

PROGRAM STEERCO
JULY, 2023

Meeting regulatory requirements requires us to transition all 105 legacy reports into the case system by the end of this financial year.

We have now reviewed plans and estimates and are ready to discuss potential ways forward.

We need to decide
to either spend
$1.2 million to
$2 million more over
the coming two
years or to
renegotiate
requirements with
the regulator

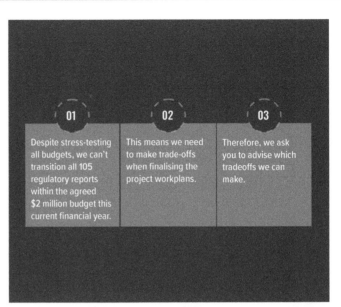

Despite stress-testing all budgets, we can't transition all 105 regulatory reports within the agreed $2 million budget this financial year

01 Updated estimates for database came back at $2m, which is 2.5 x the original budget due to a more comprehensive scoping. (See appendix for breakdown.)

02 Budgets for other aspects of the work have not materially changed. Costs for workflow, API linking, and operational aspects remain steady.

03 Work required for reports identified since June last year has not been factored in.

This means we need to make trade-offs when finalising the project workplans

Option 1

Spend $1.2m more now or $2m more later

We could deliver
- everything in FY23 with $1.2m more during FY23
- some in FY23, some in FY24 with $2m or more in total.

Option 2

Renegotiate scope or time with the regulator

We could
- limit the scope to delivering only the top 70 reports by FY23 within the current budget and negotiate with the regulator to accept this as final
- seek agreement from the regulator to further extend project timelines.

We ask you to advise which trade-offs we can make

We need to decide whether we

Spend more by
1. increasing funding by $1.2m for FY23
2. budgeting $2m more for the project in total and roll into next year.

Renegotiate by
1. accepting the top 70 reports in FY23 as adequate and convincing the regulator to agree
2. seeking extensions from the regulator.

The Regulatory Projects Steering Committee advises which trade-offs the team can make to finalise workplans for 2024.

EXECUTIVE SUMMARY

Meeting regulatory requirements requires us to transition all 105 legacy reports into the case system by the end of this financial year. We have now reviewed the plans and estimates and are ready to discuss potential ways forward.

In sum, we need to decide to either spend an extra $1.2 million to $2 million over the coming two years or renegotiate requirements with the regulator. Here is an outline of our high-level position before going into more detail below.

1. Despite stress testing all budgets, we can't transition all 105 regulatory reports within the agreed $2 million budget this financial year.
2. This means we need to make trade-offs when finalising the workplans.
3. As a result, we ask you to advise which trade-offs we can make.

DISCUSSION

Despite stress testing all budgets, we can't transition all 105 regulatory reports within the agreed $2 million budget this financial year. After conducting the thorough review that you requested, we found

- Updated estimates for database came back at $2 million – 2.5 times the original budget due to a more comprehensive scoping. (See appendix for breakdown.)
- Budgets for other aspects of the work have not materially changed. Costs for workflow, API linking, and operational aspects remain steady.
- Any reports that have been identified as needing to be reworked since June last year have not been factored into this.

This means we need to make trade-offs when finalising the workplans. Given these trade-offs require your endorsement to be implemented, we offer alternatives for your consideration.

Option 1: Spend $1.2 million more now or $2 million more later. We could then deliver either

- everything in FY23 with $1.2 million more during FY23
- some in FY23, some in FY24 with $2 million or more.

Option 2: Renegotiate scope or time with the regulator. If taking this path, we could

- limit the scope to delivering only the top 70 reports by FY23 within the current budget and negotiate with the regulator to accept this as final, or
- seek agreement from the regulator to further extend project timelines.

As a result, we ask you to advise which trade-offs we can make. This involves deciding whether to

- Spend more by either
  - increasing funding by $1.2 million for FY23, or
  - budgeting $2 million more for the project in total and roll into next year.
- Renegotiate by either
  - accepting the top 70 reports in FY23 as adequate and convincing the regulator to agree, or
  - seeking extensions from the regulator.

We understand this is not the outcome you were hoping for but look forward to your decision as to the best way forward.

ATTACHMENTS

Detailed financial breakdown of the updated financial estimates for all aspects of the 105 reports project.

SUBMITTED BY

Ryan Bloggs, Program Manager, Regulatory Projects

▲ Factor in prescriptive corporate templates if needed

Templates for business cases, updates and other reports are used widely to ensure an author has 'thought about everything'. They are often also quite detailed, telling you what topic to cover where.

They rarely form a basis for a strong narrative. Assuming that all you need to do is fill in the sections can impede your ability to engage decision-makers.

If you are fortunate, your template will allow room for an executive summary. This is 'the money spot' where you add your narrative – either just the top line structure for the story or the extra layer you will have mapped out with your team on your one pager. However, it is not always that easy.

In this section, I offer suggestions to help use message mapping alongside the key kinds of corporate templates I see in play.

This involves 'wrangling' a template to accommodate message maps in four ways:

1. *Use your message map as your executive summary.* Many templates for business cases or updates include a box for your executive summary. Some people add the message map as an image, but most insert the content in text form.

2. *Use your message map as speaking notes.* Reports may be fixed in structure, sometimes because they are automatically generated. When this happens, you may want to summarise the information in the report into a message map that you use to introduce the presentation.

You may go a step further and explain the implications of the report findings, if that is helpful.

Either way, you could include the narrative in the email that you attach the report to or deliver it verbally (ideally) before or (if necessary) after you dive into the data.

3. *Create separate mini stories for each section.* Where you have a series of topics you must cover, I suggest working out what the message for each of these points is. Add that message after the section title. Here is an example where two topics are in play for a retailer's routine leadership update:

> Sales – 12% growth driven by increased foot traffic from shopping centre campaign.

> Safety - Slips and trips remain stable at X for June with no major incidents.

These page titles can then form the substance of your executive summary. Once you line them up on a page you can stand back and ask yourself what overall message they suggest, and use that as your main message for the deck.

4. *Add an executive summary page up front.* Where this is not typically included, I suggest adding a full narrative ('What', 'Why', main message and supporting points) at the front. If in PowerPoint, this would be the first page after the title page; if in prose, then as close to the front of the document as you can get it.

Now you are comfortable with the links between a message map and a paper or presentation, let's look at how to review your own or your team's drafts.

▲ Know how to quickly review papers and presentations

Given the tight link between the message map and the document, we can revert to a tailored version of the Scan, Score, Share technique to quickly review a draft.

Here is how I do that, whether working freeform or within a corporate template.

SCAN the high-level messaging to see if it matches the map

As with the one-pager, my initial scan takes seconds.

The first thing I check is whether the document telegraphs the messaging so it is easy to find. Then I scan the structure of the messaging. I offer here the key things I look for in each case.

First: Is the messaging easy to find?

Even though I don't have the structure of the message map to guide me here, I can easily check the messaging structure other ways.

Here are the initial four questions I ask myself in conducting this quick scan:

1. Is there a short executive summary at the start that matches the message map?
2. Can I see the main message without looking hard for it?
3. Do the top-line messages stand out in larger font with more white space around them than lower-level points?
4. Can I skim the hierarchy of the messaging without reading the details?

Then I ask: Is the structure strong?

Here I am looking for very similar things as I do when reviewing a one-pager, e.g.

1. Are there two to five sections at every level?
2. If there are three points at any level, do they look grouped or deductive?
a. If grouped, do the words follow a common language pattern?
b. If deductive, is it obvious that the statement leads to the comment and then the recommendation?
3. Are the proportions right? (That is, are there any sections that seem really big while others are tiny, hinting at problems with synthesis?)

Once I have undertaken this quick scan I decide what is next. If it looks terrific, that's easy: I let the author know. If I saw problems, I decide whether to analyse further myself, or ask the team to go back to better align the document with the message map.

SCORE the document to draw out areas for improvement

If I decide to analyse further, I try to work out whether the problems are to do with the visualisation of the message, or whether the message itself has come undone.

If the problems relate to visualisation, where the message is intact but poorly represented, I ask the team to better align it with the message map. I typically offer suggestions about how to do this to guide their repair, sometimes reworking a section to illustrate.

If I fear the message itself has come undone, I revert back to the one-page message map to find the disconnect. This may involve backfilling information into the one-pager and reviewing it against the SCORE framework to check the message has maintained its integrity.

This disconnect between message and document typically occurs when the one-pager was signed off too quickly. The team has then raced off to prepare the paper or presentation without iterating back with you about the way their thinking has changed.

The challenge with refining the thinking inside the document itself is that the high-level messaging easily gets lost. This then makes the document harder to follow, requiring late changes from you.

Although late changes are hard to eradicate, focusing the work around the message map will minimise them.

SHARE your observations to help the team settle the document

There are many ways to share your observations with your team, which will be driven by practicalities all round. Here are some thoughts to help.

Choose the best mode

Your team's availability and capability will help you decide how to approach this conversation. Do you:

1. Meet to ask them to talk through the shift in messaging so you can together fine-tune the document?
2. Ask them to provide an updated message map that reflects their new thinking before you review the document?
3. Help them diagnose the thinking problems within the document by walking through the SCORE framework together?
4. Rework it yourself to better align the new messaging with the document format? (Hopefully not!)

Ultimately you will balance the amount of time everyone has before the document must be submitted with the amount of improvement needed when deciding how to proceed.

Mix clarity with tact

Regardless of your chosen path, I offer three suggestions for sharing your observations.

1. *Use message mapping language to help your team embed the concepts in their minds.* If the problem is with the main message – say so. If the 'what' is bulging, offering too much background – say so. If the ideas are not well grouped or not tightly deductive – say so.
2. *Focus on the structure and substance of the message more than the language style.* Even though we always want communication for senior audiences to *look* good, it is more important to *be* good.

   Even if your team uses a different speaking voice or illustrates things in a way that you would not, the document may still be fit for purpose.

   Everyone knows these documents are a team effort, and it is fair to ask yourself how much of your weekend you should spend making something that is substantively on point 'look and feel' like you wrote it.
3. *Tread lightly but firmly where the problems are substantial.* Here are three thoughts to help with that:

a. *Use questions to diagnose what is going on.* Unless I have explicit permission from my clients to be blunt (some prefer that!), I avoid describing the problems myself. Rather, I ask questions about the structure that lead them to see the problems themselves.

b. *Offer suggestions rather than critique.* Where someone isn't getting where I want them to go through my questioning techniques, I turn to 'what if we …' to highlight other ways of handling the draft.

c. *Ask them to walk me through the narrative verbally.* If I see big problems, I might ask them to tell me about the structure. I often find they can tell the story better than they can write it, and this saves much time. This can be faster than working through the document line by line, which can be torturous and slow when the writing (and thinking!) is muddled.

Having worked with the message map process, experience tells me less rework on the document will be required than in the past, which will release you to think more about how you actually present to your audience.

▲ Present with polish

Whatever the end deliverable looks like, you likely need to talk it through with your key stakeholders. You may need to have early-stage discussions about the narrative, present it formally, or both.

Having structured the messaging well, you want your delivery to help rather than hinder your progress.

Framing and flagging help your audience keep up with you, while flexing to their responses allows for maximum engagement. Here are ideas to help with all three.

Frame where you are going so your audience knows what to expect

Framing enables you to get above the narrative itself to explain where you are going with the discussion. It provides both you and the audience with confidence by helping you set expectations and direct the discussion.

Framing also helps your decision-makers tune in to your topic from the beginning.

Ideally, you will begin with a short recap of the paper to remind your audience what you are there to discuss. You might say something like this:

> Today I will recap on our recommendation for supporting the next phase of Project X before opening for discussion. I'll quickly set the scene and then be up-front about our recommendation before giving you our high-level thinking. Then we can work through the details together.

As an example, a senior government client of mine uses the following wonderful frame when he has to share difficult news:

> Today we are here to talk about X difficult topic. Before I start, I want you to know that I have some bad news and some good news, but it will be all right in the end.

This is particularly useful when you have used the Oh Dear pattern, which opens by introducing a problem that is new to your audience.

Carefully done, this can engage your audience in a new problem and prepare them to hear your recommended solution.

Care is, however, paramount with this pattern and framing helps with that.

Flag where you are up to so your audience can keep up

Let your audience know each time you transition from one section of the structure to the next.

Your flag can be as simple as saying, 'Now to my third point: risks'. Or, perhaps something like 'Now that we have covered off on how this recommendation aligns with our overall strategy, I'll share our thoughts on the returns'.

I keep flags general, describing what I am talking about rather than what I am saying.

Flex to your audience's responses for maximum engagement

Although confidence in your ability to present your paper or PowerPoint is important, you may not need to present as much as you think. Ideally, your decision-makers will already have read your paper. They usually prefer to have a discussion than just listen and may be short on time.

Many a group has found that their audience doesn't want to discuss their topic in the same way they do. You might be ready to make a recommendation for a new approach, while they might want to talk to you in depth about changes in the industry, or perhaps revisit key issues from the previous meeting.

In these instances, you have little choice but to address their issues first. Once these are settled, you will have an appreciative audience, but be short on time.

Equally, many a group has been allocated 30 minutes in a senior meeting only to be squeezed to just five as previous presentations have run over time. The worst thing to do at this point is to assume you need to speak fast to 'cover everything'.

Let me share an example here to illustrate how to handle this common challenge.

After a whole-day board meeting, 'Mary's exec team came together at 6 pm, which was an hour later than planned, for a one-hour meeting to discuss three issues.

Mary drew the short straw: she was third out of the three and now looking to present to an exhausted leadership at about 6.50 pm.

As the meeting progressed, each of her peers began with something like this:

> 'I realise it's been a long day, so I'll keep it short'.

They then did the opposite, taking the leaders on a convoluted journey through every detail of their presentation and working toward the big reveal at the end.

If the leaders were tired at the start of the meeting, their minds were now 'mush'.

Mary's solution was to share the high-level messaging using the executive summary as her guide.

Within five minutes she had her approval and a grateful exec team in her corner after three questions.

Her comment afterwards was that the thinking she and her team did to prepare the message map was the key. Being clear about the story in her own mind enabled her to cover the high-level ideas quickly, insightfully and calmly.

This is a story I have heard time and again, even though some clients worry they are spending too much time thinking up-front.

Now you can see how to use the message map when preparing your communication, it is time to embed the learning from this new process into the team's ways of working.

In the next chapter, I offer ideas for hardwiring feedback into your regular rhythm so you and your team can keep improving, presentation by presentation.

CHAPTER 6

Embed the learning to create a positive flywheel effect

A significant missed opportunity arises when you don't take a few moments to reflect on what went well, what didn't and what you can do differently next time.

This step is often ignored as everyone moves quickly from one task to the next.

It can be hard to remember to take five minutes to capitalise on what everyone learned from a paper or presentation. It can also be consciously avoided for fear of having difficult conversations. Communication can be perceived as being more personal than some other aspects of work, which can magnify this fear.

I offer questions as thought starters to help you and the team take the insights gleaned from one paper into future papers and presentations.

For the most part, these conversations can be quick, focusing on 'What did we learn that can help us next time?'.

If they become burdensome, they will quickly fall by the wayside.

Keep it simple by cherry picking which are the most relevant opportunities to improve together by:

▲ Assessing the quality of conversation stimulated by the paper or presentation.
▲ Better understanding stakeholder needs and preferences.
▲ Capturing reactions to the presentation itself.
▲ Optimising forward collaboration.

The following sections include some questions to stimulate your thinking in each of these areas.

▲ Assess the quality of conversation stimulated by the paper or presentation

It should come as no surprise that not all conversations are equally valuable and that different people bring different perspectives to those conversations.

Even if you were the one to present your team's paper in the meeting, you may pick up on different things than your colleagues and team mates, so it's worth unpacking this a bit. Here are some questions to help flush that out:

▲ What proportion of the discussion was spent clarifying the ideas in the paper rather than discussing its substance?

▲ Was the conversation polarised toward one or two vocal people, or did everyone participate?

▲ Were these the subject matter experts or others with loud voices?

▲ Did you get a valuable answer from the group, even if it wasn't the one you wanted?

If the conversation was deeply focused on the material issues and involved many people on the decision-making group, you can be confident the paper did its job. This doesn't mean it couldn't have been better, but it is a good sign.

▲ Better understand stakeholder needs and preferences

Every time you engage with someone or a group, you learn more about their preferences. Here are a couple of questions to consolidate your learnings with your team:

▲ What did you learn about stakeholders' positions and strategies in relation to this topic?

▲ Did any stakeholders have a strong view one way or another about the issue?

▲ Did any stakeholders seem less interested than you expected?

▲ Have any stakeholders shifted their perspectives since last time?

Individuals and groups change over time, so even if you think you have a good understanding of the group, be alert to shifts.

▲ Capture reactions to the presentation itself

When thinking about the reactions to the presentation, focus on the quality and the structure of the content. Here are some thought starters:

▲ Did anyone comment about the quality of the paper (or not)?

▲ What worked well regarding the substance and the structure of the paper or presentation?

▲ Did you and your team miss any key messages?

▲ Did the framing work?

▲ What did stakeholders suggest you and your team do differently next time?

▲ Optimise forward collaboration

The quality of the outcome may be aligned with the quality of the process. Take a few moments to reflect on how the process itself went with your team:

▲ Did you receive the message maps and the documents with sufficient time to review them?

▲ Did anyone try to sneak the document through without a corresponding stakeholder analysis, outcome statement and message map?

▲ Did the team pay sufficient attention to the quality of the thinking before sending it to you for review?

▲ Did the team peer-review the message map and, separately, the document before sending to you for review?

I hope these questions and thought starters are useful, and I look forward now to helping you elevate your team's skills.

We have covered quite some ground. Now it's time to lift your team's capabilities so they can deliver higher quality thinking in their papers and presentations ... and so you need to rewrite them much less than you do now.

PART III

Elevate the team

CHAPTER 7

Engage the team in the new ways of working

Now you are comfortable with building your own message maps, it is time to engage the team in this new way of thinking and working.

You will first need to build momentum, so team members are motivated to change their approach for major communication. They need to have a purpose to believe in and see no alternative but to change. Here are the steps I suggest you take.

▲ Involve high-performing team members first
▲ Warm up the broader team
▲ Encourage concrete steps.

Let's now did into each one.

▲ Involve high-performing team members first

I suggest first involving one or two high-performing team members.

This provides you with thought partners and later, will spread the coaching load. It also helps the word trickle out more broadly across the team.

The team will see you thinking through your messaging or be asked to contribute to a message map. They will notice something different is afoot and with some careful management, they will become curious. They might even feel some FOMO (fear of missing out).

They may also see standards and expectations lift, which is important in any change effort. They will start to feel the need to improve.

This is more important with communication than with some other areas. The Dunning Kruger[1] effect is

---

1   The Dunning–Kruger effect is a cognitive bias where people with limited knowledge or competence in an area overestimate their knowledge or competence relative to objective criteria or to the performance of peers or other people in general.

strong here. Many executives are unaware of what is possible and how poor their communication is.

This is, in my experience, for many reasons. Here are two. Quality feedback is in short supply and leaders too often rework their team's communication without explaining why they make specific changes.

So, let's fix both those things.

▲ Warm up the broader team

I suggest building momentum with the broader team in two phases by initially warming your team up to the opportunity before being more specific about what's coming.

Building an understanding of the problem and the opportunity allows you to build momentum while building your own skills and plans in parallel. Being candid about your own experiences as well as those of your stakeholders is an easy way to start that doesn't require much effort. Let's go there first before intentionally motivating the team.

Seek and share explicit feedback from your team's stakeholders

Ask these stakeholders to 'not hold back' in their assessments of where your team's papers could improve. Here are some questions to seed your conversations:

▲ Are papers easy to understand? If not, how many times do they read your team's papers before they understand them? How long does this take?

▲ Are papers substantively on point, or are they hard to navigate and 'not quite there' in terms of the quality of insights?

▲ How do they describe the consequences of these problems?
  – Would discussions be more insightful if pre-reading was better?
  – Could better decisions be made, perhaps also more quickly?
  – How else could better papers and presentations help lift the quality of our meetings?

Share the outcomes of these conversations with your team so they can see the cost and the opportunity. Even better: ask a prominent stakeholder to spend

10 minutes sharing their observations and views of the opportunities with the team.

This then provides you with specific material that enables you to become more targeted in your feedback to the team. When you review or rework a paper, take the time to be specific about your observations. What is working? What is not?

Start talking through your experience with the team's papers

Now is time to start salting existing conversations with some observations, ideas and questions to raise awareness.

Share your own thinking about the communication cost for you and the team. Wherever you can, also ask questions. I find it gets people thinking in a way that 'telling' doesn't.

Here are four ideas to start the team thinking about both the problem and the opportunity.

Cement the problem you are addressing

Ask your team questions to help them come to terms with the situation in a way that makes it real to them. Here are four possibilities:

1. Can you think of a recent piece of communication that led to poor decision-making?

2. What did that mean? Was the decision itself suboptimal? Slow in coming, or even absent?
3. What were the consequences for the business and for our team?
4. How many iterations did we make for that paper? How long did it take? Who delayed other priority tasks or worked outside regular hours to get it done?

Size the prize

Again, I prefer to go with questions when honing in on benefits for the team. Here are five examples:

1. What would happen if we were able to craft communication that was approved with no (or little) adjustment at every step of the chain?
2. What would be the consequences for us and the broader business?
3. How would we measure that?
4. How much time would that return to us over an average week?
5. What would it feel like to routinely have our papers approved by decision-makers 'first go'?

'Feel it', don't just 'know it'

In salting these conversations, focus on the facts as well as the feelings that come from success. Hearing client success stories doesn't just excite me because they spend their time better at work and get better results. They excite me because of the human impact. When Cerise and Jason told me their stories, for example, they felt like winners.

Cerise manages a substantial portfolio of projects for a large bank. She was thrilled to be asked by one of her peers how she gets pretty much every paper approved first go. They did not think that was possible, yet she was confidently 'landing' her papers each time.

Jason was thrilled when one of his team had taken the initiative to learn the message map approach on his own before handing him a one-pager he could approve in minutes. At that stage, he hadn't seen the approach in action but loved that he could review and respond so quickly. His junior was also thrilled to have such a fast response.

Imagine what these kinds of wins would feel like for you and your team. Use examples like these to get your team also imagining what it would feel like.

Lock in the WIIFM (what's in it for me?)

If your team members want to move above a technical role, they need to not just get the right answer but they also need to connect the dots between the technical and commercial aspects of their work.

As management guru Peter Drucker said in his 2013 book *People and Performance*:

As soon as you move one step up from the bottom, your effectiveness depends on your ability to reach others through the spoken and written word.

Having started to talk about your new ideas about communication, it is time to draw the team into your thinking by becoming specific about your hopes and expectations.

▲ Encourage concrete steps

Your team will be coming from many directions.

For some, this way of thinking and communicating will align with their current ways of working. For others, it will be a stretch.

Some will be accustomed to incrementally improving their predecessors' communication and think that is good enough. Others will be nervous about expressing a point of view, either because they are not sure how to do that or they might see that as your job.

Here are two further ideas to encourage your team to lean into the process and make a big shift in the quality of their communication, whatever their current mindset.

Encourage the team to express a point of view, not just facts

They may find this liberating! Many feel hamstrung by templates and processes and do not feel at liberty to offer their opinion.

When working with the finance team from an Australian retailer recently, for example, I was delighted with the reaction from some of the team. They were shocked that they were allowed to offer a point of view rather than just the data. They were excited about that prospect because it gave their work more meaning.

Even if the team is off base with their ideas, having a conversation around that helps you both. You will see where they are coming from and have an opportunity to coach them.

Be ready to answer questions

While I find that teams readily enjoy the benefits of the new way of working, some will come with questions. Three in particular can be tricky to tackle, so

I outline them here and offer potential answers.

'This new way of writing seems all well and good, but it's just one way. Why can't I get there in my own way?'

In your reply, acknowledge that the person is right that it is possible to write many different ways. This approach, however, is as much about thinking and collaborating as it is about writing. It may help to explain the differences:

- Message mapping helps with clarity and collaboration. It gives us a consistent language and approach for working together when preparing a wide range of communication. Consistency makes the process faster and easier for us all.

- It pushes us to think harder about our messaging. The process itself helps us focus on the big ideas first, writing second. I haven't found another method that does that.

- Message maps help stakeholders contribute. Other approaches don't offer fast ways for stakeholders, including me, to provide you with valuable insights into your messaging.

- The approach matches leadership expectations. They want us to deliver our key messaging early and then back up with the details. It gives them choices in how they read the material, which no other approach does.

'How will I fit learning this new approach into my day? I am already slammed.'

Respond with something like, 'We always have too much to do. If we don't make engaging our decision-makers a priority, we will continue to be busy but be less likely to meet our KPIs.'

'My communication is different because I only communicate via templates. Why do I need to change?'

In your response, acknowledge that you can see the challenge with templates but want to encourage your team member to focus on the thinking principles that underpin this approach. Clarity of thought expressed as a single high-quality message is useful everywhere.

When it comes to templates, encourage your team member to think about each section as a mini narrative with its own mini main message.

You may also highlight that all team members contribute to sections of each others' papers, contribute during meetings and write emails. All of these situations can benefit from structured thinking.

Now the word is out there, it's time to think about the best way to build the team's capabilities.

CHAPTER 8

Lift your team's capability

Now that you have built some momentum with your team, it's time to help them build their skills too.

In this chapter, I help you make the learning matter to your team, choose your preferred skill-building approach, gather your resources and then when you are ready, lead the learning effort.

Let's work through these steps one by one.

▲ Make the learning matter to your team

Like any change management effort, it is tempting to just 'go'. Before you do that, the team needs confidence that this really matters, which means you need to explain why it matters.

Having already starting building momentum, they should be like ripe fruit and need little effort to 'harvest'.

To help with that harvest, I offer the IMPACT framework coined by my collaborator Richard Medcalf. Richard introduces this aptly named six-step framework in his excellent book *Making Time for Strategy*.

He has identified six key areas that, when lacking, become barriers to individuals and teams taking action:

- ▲ *I:* Insight
- ▲ *M:* Motivation
- ▲ *P:* Prompts
- ▲ *A:* Ability
- ▲ *C:* Consequences
- ▲ *T:* Time

In the following sections, I offer strategies for countering these potential barriers as you motivate the team to build their skills.

Insight: Describe where you want message mapping to be used

Clarifying exactly where you want your team to apply the approach now and in the future is important. This avoids ambiguity and the potential for excuses when they don't apply it when you would prefer that they did.

So, do you want them to:

▲ start with shorter communication – for example, emails and meeting contributions – as practice and then level up to major papers?

▲ focus on major papers and see the trickle-down effect for other simpler communication?

Whether you start big or small, I encourage you to first focus on the team's effort and later their achievement. Simply 'doing it' leads to increased achievement over time.

Motivation: Keep reminding them why you are doing this

Simon Sinek didn't write *Start with Why* for no reason. It's the single most overlooked word at work. It is too easy to assume that others know why we are doing something and too easy to forget to ask why.

So, make sure you are crystal clear about the following three things and repeat, repeat, repeat:

1. Why are you driving this project?
2. How will it benefit you, the team and the organisation?
3. Do you aim to optimise 'okay' performance or help the team make big steps to meet expectations?

Prompts: Explain how you will help keep them on track

Embedding message mapping into your day-to-day work will be easier if the team has reminders and tools. Consider the following prompts:

▲ Include message mapping as an item in your regular team meetings. This could involve celebrating effort or success, showcasing examples, hosting a quick quiz or some other practical reminders.

▲ Keep the concepts visual by downloading materials from my site or creating posters or other visuals to have around the office or on the team's screensavers.

▲ House templates and example documents on a SharePoint page or in a Teams channel.

▲ Modify business case and other templates to incorporate message maps overall or within sections.

These prompts will serve you well now and as you set the team up to thrive into the future.

Ability: Include skill-building time in the team's quarterly plan

Agree whether the team will commit a specific time each week for learning (for example, Monday from 1 to 2 pm for the coming month) or whether you want them to decide for themselves when their learning will happen.

Either way, check in regularly to hold them to their commitments, particularly after a couple of weeks have progressed. Motivation can dip as they realise the approach can be challenging, if they have not had a major communication to work on, or when other high priority tasks risk derailing their focus.

Consequences: Deliver consequences so everyone stays on track

You will see some intrinsic pay-offs here, especially at the start. These are unlikely to be sufficient for some of your team, though, particularly after the initial enthusiasm rubs off and they need to think harder about their communication.

Those who struggle to use the ideas, who did not pay full attention to their learning or who are jaded are at risk. Solve this by sticking to your commitment to reject first drafts they provide in any format other than a one-page message map.

As my client Anthony Wilson, the previous head of risk and compliance at a major Australian retailer said, you will only need to do it once.

Time: Explain why this matters now

Explain why improving papers and presentations matters now. Perhaps you've chosen this timeline for one (or more) of the following reasons:

▲ You're introducing the approach during a lull in the normal working rhythm.

▲ You've decided to charge forward because there is never a good time, so why not now?

▲ You've received recent feedback from leadership that the papers need to improve.

▲ You've realised that skills need to lift to tackle a particular upcoming task.

Whatever your reason and timeline, make sure your team is aware of it.

Once you have started the team moving forward, it's time to build their skills.

▲ Choose your skill-building approach

Building your team's skills is, of course, challenging amid the seemingly infinite number of operational tasks you can be dragged into.

To make that easier for you, I offer three potential 'leader-led' skill-building strategies, along with an explanation of the benefits and drawbacks of each. You might choose to coach them on a just-in-time basis, host a 'Clarity Club' to help them learn as a group, or go further and facilitate a short, practical workshop.

Let's now look at these options so you can decide what will best suit your circumstances and ambition.

Offer 'just in time' coaching to kick-start a small group

You could adopt this approach in two ways.

Option 1. You could coach your team step by step as you prepare each upcoming paper or presentation. My free PowerPoint Planner[1] will help guide your process.

This suits smart teams of conceptual thinkers. It relies on you thinking ahead so you can explain the concepts while problem-solving important papers.

Option 2. Alternatively, you may offer them an opportunity to learn first by offering one of the following:

▲ *My companion book, Engage,* takes your team through the Elevate process. It introduces the approach and offers 12 detailed case studies sharing how each of the 10 patterns have played out in real life. It is deliberately practical and short, and aligns with *Elevate.*

▲ *My latest self-paced course by the same name:* My self-paced online courses are deeper than the books. They revolve around short modules supplemented by challenge questions, downloadable notes and supplementary material.

You can learn more about both of these at ClarityFirstProgram.com.

Once your team is across the concepts, you can guide them through the message mapping process.

Host a 'Clarity Club' to introduce the ideas to a larger group

Explaining something to someone else is a great way to boost our own ability.

---

1   www.ClarityFirstProgram.com/ClarityHub

Using my step-by-step guide, you can build your team's skills while enhancing your own over four weeks.

This approach is effective for any group, large or small, whether conceptual or analytical thinkers. All it requires is the plan, access to either *Engage* or the online modules, and a commitment to the time and learning.

You, or one of your champions, will shepherd the process. This involves preparing for and facilitating the learning as well as allowing time for the team to compete any pre-work homework, attend the session and experiment with the ideas.

Facilitate a short, practical workshop to concentrate the skill-building

You may like to go further than a Clarity Club and run a short workshop for your team, with or without the support of *Engage* or my online modules.

Leaders who enjoy facilitating may find this attractive. It will stretch you (or your champions who facilitate) to have a deeper level of skill that will benefit you all.

This is true whether you develop your own materials or choose to use mine.

Although more demanding, this approach can be rewarding for all. Whichever approach you choose, you will need resources.

▲ Gather your resources

I offer downloadable templates and tools to help you bring this approach to life with your team.

I split the free options into two parts. The core toolkit for building message maps and the leaders' kit, which is just for you.

I also offer a separate and paid Workshop Kit for those who would prefer not to prepare their own examples and exercises.

I introduce them here so you can work out what works best for you and your team.

The Core Toolkit offers essentials

My Toolkit includes the basics to help you and your team build your skills as you implement message mapping. Here's what is included with your one month's free access to the online Clarity Hub[2].

Skill-building tools

The core kit offers two key tools to help you build your team's skills:

- ▲ A 10-minute mini-course explaining how to use these ideas for emails. Your team can register using this link: ClarityFirstProgram.com/emails.
- ▲ Monthly MasterClasses on a range of communication topics. Topics have included Understanding Boards and Making Updates Interesting. Hub members can propose topics for future sessions also.

Implementation tools

It also includes four tools to help you put the ideas into practice across your team:

- ▲ The PowerPoint Planner to guide you and your team as you think through your communication.
- ▲ The SCORE framework for providing feedback on your team's papers.
- ▲ The Pattern Picker to help you decide which message map suits your needs best. This offers more nuance than I have included in this book. It invites you to answer a series of questions that

will lead you to download the message map and instructions for your chosen pattern.

- ▲ A deck of 25 pre-made hard-to-create images and diagrams to use inside your PowerPoint presentations.

This may be sufficient, or alternatively you may like extra tools for leading your program.

The Leaders' Toolkit offers extra support

You may like extra tips and tools to help you lead your team. I offer downloads and guides that you will need to lead your team in this separate toolkit.

The Leaders' Toolkit includes the following to help you deliver whichever skill-building approach you choose.

- ▲ Clarity Club guide to support your discussions.
- ▲ One-page Workshop planner to guide you through the workshop approach.
- ▲ A video to help 'hack your templates'. Marrying your message mapping strategy with pre-defined templates is easy when you know how.

---

2   ClarityFirstProgram.com/ClarityHub

The Workshop Kit avoids reinventing the wheel

If you're planning a workshop to train your team but would prefer not to build your own exercises and examples, I offer a fully annotated Workshop Kit for a fixed fee.

It includes everything you need to facilitate a successful workshop, including these five things:

▲ PowerPoint slides to introduce concepts and run exercises across a three-hour workshop and coaching sessions

▲ A facilitator's guide, including video guides and frequently asked questions

▲ Tools and templates for you all

▲ Annotated templates for prose board papers and emails

▲ Annotated PowerPoints showcasing the approach in play for live communication.

▲ Lead the learning

Your leadership and coaching will be foundational to shifting your team's communication ability over time.

Although tempting, a 'one and done' approach to learning is ineffective. This is one of the many reasons I wrote this book. So much is lost after the workshop if the approach is not embedded on a day-to-day basis.

The key principles I encourage you to adopt are:

▲ Introduce the ideas in small chunks to allow them to sink in. Introducing too much at once means ideas get lost in the clutter of day-to-day busyness.

▲ Allow time for your team to iterate between learning and doing so the ideas shift from 'concept' to 'practice'.

Good ideas aren't enough on their own if they are not used.

▲ Recognise that old habits are there to be broken ... and the team will revert to old habits when under pressure unless kept on track.

▲ You will need both carrots and sticks.

You may have already chosen your approach.

Here's a mini index to help you jump straight to the relevant section.

Offer just-in-time coaching

While I encourage you to offer everyone a copy of *Engage*, you may also like to explain the approach yourself. Here are some thoughts to guide you.

Introduce the approach

You will need to explain what a message map is and how to use one. Here are some thoughts to guide that discussion.

Explain that this approach enables everyone to collaborate more effectively to deliver higher-quality insights that engage key decision-makers. Highlight how message mapping:

▲ helps you brief them effectively and early so they have greater autonomy in preparing the papers, reducing rework for all

▲ anchors around a structured one-page map of our ideas rather than a template to 'fill in'

▲ enables everyone to work out the single main message, or insight, that will engage our stakeholders

▲ helps order supporting points in a highly structured way.

You may like to share the following three key slides with them to explain how it works. I have added them here as thumbnails as you are already familiar with them and can download them full-size from the Clarity Hub.

Slides to help your team

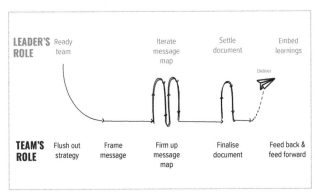

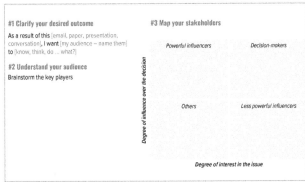

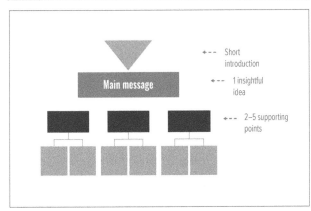

Once they have a basic sense of the framework, start collaborating around the communication.

Ready them for a specific paper or presentation

Five things will help you and the team to think through the communication strategy and high-level structure for the communication:

1. Share the schedule for the relevant paper or presentation.
2. Help them understand the desired outcome and audience before sketching out the high-level message map with them. Once their skills are advanced, they will be able to sketch out the message maps themselves.
3. Ask them to fill in any gaps in the initial draft message map that you create together and provide the draft back to you in time for your review.
4. Be explicit about time frames to reduce the chance that you end up rewriting the paper regardless.
5. Give them permission to experiment and get it wrong. Even if they muck it up terribly the first few times, they will progress further faster if they are not 'cut down' for experimenting and then making mistakes.

The PowerPoint Planner will help you guide this session, step by step.

Allow a generous amount of time to iterate the message map together

The first few reviews will take longer, while the team is coming to understand how the approach works. Allow time to:

1. Explain why you want to change any areas of their message map. Don't stop at explaining 'what' needs to change. Helping your team understand 'why' changes are needed increases the chance they can deliver something better next time.
2. Be open to running multiple sessions for the first few papers to give the team time to think through their material and how to 'work it' into a message map. This will be most important if the early examples are complicated.
3. Demonstrate how to flip a message map into a document. You may want to do this together the first time or two.

Even though the first few papers will take longer, you will get the time back over subsequent communication. You can also encourage the team to practice ideas for simpler communication such as emails.

Meet to settle the document

In these early stages, sitting down in person or online is more helpful than working via email. At a minimum, if you need to use email, supplement that email with a phone call so you can clarify any misunderstandings. I encourage you to be detailed as you work with your team members to make sure the hierarchy of the thinking matches the hierarchy of the document.

Refer back to chapter 5 where I go into settling the document in more detail.

Take the time to embed the learnings with the team

Ask stakeholders for their feedback and share it. Share your own observations of what it was like to present their paper. Include any positives and don't hold back on areas for further improvement. This is a journey and even if the first attempt is perfect, it is likely that future ones will have areas for improvement.

Host a 'Clarity Club'

A Clarity Club offers a fast and effective way to get your team started as they together work through either *Engage* or my online course. The online course covers the same concepts at greater depth, but either option is effective. It really depends on how your team prefers to learn and how far you want your team's skills to progress.

You will have already decided what learning resources will work best for you and hopefully downloaded the team guides from the Clarity Hub Leaders' Toolkit.

Let's now walk through how the four-week Clarity Club works, week by week being guided by the program to the right.

Week minus 1: Decide how to structure the club

Here are some structuring ideas:

- ▲ *Decide how often you want to meet:* You may like to meet weekly to keep the cadence up while allowing time for practice and discussion between sessions. Alternatively, you may prefer to power through more quickly to accommodate a lull in your workload or to add extra energy and focus. Equally, a more drawn-out cadence of fortnightly meetings may suit your team better. Try not to leave more than two weeks between sessions for the sake of momentum.
- ▲ *Allow enough time for discussion:* I've structured the guide so you can choose how deep you want to go into each

Clarity Club Plan

Week 0 Get started	Week 1 Clarify outcome	Week 2 Use patterns	Week 3 Firm up messaging	Week 4 Settle documents
0	**01**	**02**	**03**	**04**
> Explain why you are doing this > Confirm logistics, allowing about an hour each week for individual learning and time to practice on live work. > Provide PowerPoint Planner to all > Set homework – Ask them to read the introduction plus chapters 1, 2 & 3 of the *Engage* book or complete all Foundation & Strategy modules from the *Engage* course	**Reflect –** > Message mapping process > Stakeholder needs > Desired outcome **Ask –** > Where have you understood stakeholders well? Where have you not? > Where could you use the ideas next? > Insights so far? **Challenge –** > Map key stakeholders for a current communication **Extend –** > Read Chapter 4 of *Engage* or complete the Frame Your Messaging modules from the online course > Practise with first email every day	**Reflect –** > Patterns as useful short cut **Ask –** > Where have you tried a pattern? Which one? > Which ones might become your 'go to'? **Challenge –** > Pick a pattern and use it to draft an email > Use a pattern to sketch out a message map together **Extend –** > Read Chapter 5 of *Engage* or complete the Firm Up Your Messaging modules from the online course. > Build and peer review a message map for a live communication	**Reflect –** > First principles help squeeze out the insights **Ask –** > Have you used SCORE yet? > Have you collaborated to build a message map? > Can you share an example? **Challenge –** > Scan and SCORE a one-page message map > Scan and SCORE an email first and then a more complex doc **Extend –** > Complete remaining chapters or modules from *Engage* > Require message maps for all future papers	**Reflect –** > Your observations of changes in emails and other docs **Ask –** > Have you completed a whole map to doc cycle? > What templates do we need to adjust? **Challenge –** > Review the prose and PowerPoint examples **Extend –** > Decide how to handle templates so they align with message mapping principles > See chapter 9 in *Elevate* for ideas for you and your champions to embed the approach into the longer term

topic. You may like to vary the time allowed topic by topic or be consistent for all sessions. Here are some ideas to help you decide what you could achieve in different time frames:

1. *One hour:* Time enough to recap the topic, discuss people's impressions of the section and review examples of people's 'experiments' from the past week.

2. *90 minutes to 2 hours:* Add time for a challenge. Work on a stakeholder strategy, rework a piece of communication or build a rough skeleton for a new one.

▲ *Ground the sessions in reality by discussing concrete examples:* Develop a library of examples you could focus on, potentially collecting past examples as reference. You may like to call the sessions 'clarity sessions' or something similar to keep everyone's minds focused on outcomes.

Week 0: Get started

Now it's time to get started.

This is your opportunity to explain why you are supporting your team to strengthen their structured thinking skills. Revert to the IMPACT framework from the start of this chapter for your key points

and set the logistics in play. Equally, here are some words that might help:

Message mapping offers a structured way to collaborate that will produce better papers more quickly. It:
- *drives clarity of thinking and communication*
- *supports faster and better decision-making at all levels*
- *underwrites a culture of intelligent collaboration around real issues*
- *builds credibility and trust within the team and with decision-makers.*
Some describe the process as an 'insight engine'. It is a tool or perhaps a machine that helps us think, if we trust the structures.

Once you have explained why you will be doing this, set the club in motion:

▲ Agree on a homework schedule with the team, potentially following the weekly plan outlined here. Perhaps provide everyone with a copy of the club guide and ask them to start learning one of two ways:

1. Read up to and including chapter 3 of *Engage*. These chapters highlight the opportunity, introduce the high-level message mapping process and explain how to flush out your communication strategy.

2. Watch the introductory modules of the online course up to and including the module on communication strategy.

▲ Provide your team with my PowerPoint Planner and encourage them to focus heavily on the stakeholder mapping sections in the coming week.

▲ Lock in meeting times into everyone's diaries. This might seem like a small detail but it shows commitment.

Week 1: Ready the team early to clarify your desired outcome

This week you and the team focus on three early sections of *Engage*: how to think differently about your communication, how to iterate fast and early around your top-line messaging and how to flush out your strategy before you write anything.

I suggest using the RACE framework to structure this and the other discussions:

▲ Reflect and recap on concepts.

▲ Ask questions.

▲ Challenge the team to use the ideas.

▲ Extend the team's learning into the coming week.

Here's how that would play out for Week 1.

Reflect on the past week and recap the topic

Start by focusing on what the team has learned and how they have used the ideas so far.

Firstly, I encourage you to reward effort loudly and often, while not holding back on your observations if people backslide. This is unlikely at this early stage, but may occur later as the novelty wears off.

Be specific about what you have seen, calling out those who are 'giving it a go'. At this early stage, your team's efforts don't need to be perfect; they just need to happen. By 'having a go', your team will start thinking differently and making progress. 'Doing' will speed their learning even when they initially do a fairly poor job of it.

For the sake of economy, I won't raise the reward point for every session but do recommend you congratulate and celebrate whenever you see something worthy of it throughout the project. At the early stages, you may want to praise adherence to process, if you aren't seeing the results in the communication itself. This makes it even more important to keep people moving forward.

Secondly, recap the topic to focus everyone's minds. Here is a quick rundown for this session.

In the first part of the program, we need to allow time to think before we put pen to paper. This can be hard because sometimes it feels faster to dive straight into preparing the document. Experience says, however, it's not the case, particularly for major communication.

So today, we'll focus on the preparatory work – remembering how the message mapping process works and investing time to think through our strategy.

By the end of this session, we want to be clear on how to clarify our desired outcome in line with having a solid understanding of our stakeholders' needs.

Thirdly, point them to the tools they have at their disposal. The two key pages from the PowerPoint Planner to the right will help.

Ask questions to stimulate discussion

This focuses first on strategising – the work you and your team do before you write anything. So here are some questions to stimulate discussion around the first leg of the message map framework:

▲ Can you think of a time when you have invested deeply in this area? What happened with that communication?

▲ What is the next communication you will think through using these prompts?

▲ Have you now mapped your most important stakeholders according to who they are, what they care about and their style?

▲ What insights have emerged so far?

Challenge them to use the ideas – map key stakeholders together

As a leader, you have valuable insights to share about key stakeholders. Here are a few thought starters for you:

▲ Do your key stakeholders have hot topics, particular interests or concerns that your team should be aware of?

▲ Are their priorities at odds with your team's, which creates tension that must be carefully navigated?

▲ Do you know much about how they like information presented? Do they like detail? Do they like to engage personally or prefer to read? How important is pre-reading to them?

Some leaders like to hold this information close to their chest, but I encourage you to share openly with your team. This will empower them to deliver effective communication without you rewriting it.

Use my PowerPoint Planner to help them remember to be very specific about their desired outcome and to dig deeply into their audience.

To the right I offer the key strategy pages again for reference. The first helps you think through your stakeholders in the general sense and the second offers prompting questions should your stakeholders be against your proposition.

I realise you have seen these previously, but want you to be able to follow the process without flipping to and from other sections.

You may like to save these in a central file that maps out the key 'hot buttons' for your most important stakeholders.

Extend the team's learning into the coming week

▲ Set homework on the basic ideas that govern message maps, focusing first on patterns. Set the following, depending on the resource you are using:

1. *Engage* book– read chapter 4, where I introduce the idea of patterns, my 10 favourites and how to use them. This is a substantial chapter, illustrating how the approach has been used in a comprehensive set of real-world situations.
2. *Engage* course – complete the module framing your message using patterns.

▲ Start building habits. Ask your team to focus on their first email of the day, ensuring it has a single message near the start.

Communication strategy slides to help your team

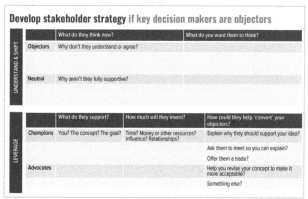

Week 2: Frame your message using patterns as a quick start

I hope you have already seen a difference in your team's communication now that they are spending more time thinking through their desired outcome.

Now it's time to get into the 'meat and potatoes' of the structure itself.

I will again frame the session using the RACE framework I used for Week 1: Reflect, Ask, Challenge and Extend.

Reflect on the past week and recap on using patterns as a quick start

Be specific in your comments about the week's progress and, wherever possible, reward effort before recapping on this week's topic. You can use the following as a sample script for your recap:

This week we focus on using patterns to draft your message map.

The 10 patterns provide examples of how we might organise our ideas. Starting with patterns helps us work intuitively so we don't (yet!) need to be experts in the mechanics of message maps.

In general, message mapping encourages us to have a super-short introduction that draws our audience toward one single main message. This message is then supported by a small number of logically organised supporting points.

Today, we'll use patterns as a way to start iterating on the message map. These are not the only structures you can use, but they do cover a lot of

ground and help us start to untangle our thinking quickly.

Ask questions to stimulate discussion

Here are questions to ask your team during this week's Club¬

- ▲ Have you tried using a pattern with or without the Pattern Picker framework (to the right for your reference)?
- ▲ Where do you see opportunities for us to use some of the patterns?
- ▲ Can you share an example with everyone, or the person sitting next to you? What worked? What didn't? Why?
- ▲ Are certain patterns likely to become our 'go-to' patterns for specific tasks? Why would they suit that task best?

Challenge the team by using the approach together

I encourage you to use these sessions to progress real tasks rather than making them academic. Here are a couple of ideas:

- ▲ Allow 30 minutes or more for the team to work in pairs or threes to pick a pattern and write an email. Ask them to share their message maps so they can learn from each other.
- ▲ Sketch out a message map for an upcoming communication as a group. This might be an update, recommendation or some other fairly routine type of communication.

Pattern Picker framework as reference

1 – CLARIFY OUTCOME	2 – REVIEW POTENTIAL MESSAGES	3 – FIND MESSAGE		4 – FRAME MESSAGE
I need my audience to ...	**To achieve that I must explain ...**	**... then pick a pattern**		**... and structure it**
> Action > Endorse > Implement > Support	Action plans How to proceed	Nike	**Do X to fix Y**	2 to 5 steps ordered by sequence or scale
> Know > Understand	Findings What analysis revealed	Nugget	**We found X**	2 to 5 points of evidence ordered by scale of importance
> Have confidence > Trust	Updates The status is green, project is going well	All is Well	**We are in good shape**	2 to 5 reasons why we are in good shape, ordered by task or time
> Agree > Approve > Change > Decide > Endorse	Strategies How to capture a new opportunity	Golden	**Do X to capture opportunity A**	Opportunity A is attractive, X will capture it, so do X
	How to solve a problem or capture an opportunity	Make the Case	**Doing X will fix Y**	2 to 5 reasons explaining why X is the right way to fix Y
	How to solve a problem that is new to your audience	Oh Dear	**Do X to solve problem Y**	Problem Y matters, but X will fix it, so do X
	Options Which options to evaluate	Short List	**Consider these for solving Y**	2 to 5 reasons to consider these options
	Best way to capture an opportunity or solve a problem	This or That	**Option X offers best approach**	We explored these options for solving Y, but option X is best, so implement X
	Improvements How to address an emerging opportunity or risk	Change Tack	**Make a change to reach goal**	Have made progress, but need to make a change to reach goal, so make a change
	How to succeed when you meet only some necessary criteria	Top up	**Top up to succeed at Y**	Succeeding at Y requires X, but we have only some of X in place, so top up

I suggest avoiding anything too substantial yet so you can focus on structuring the ideas rather than being derailed by solving the problem itself. You might use my PowerPoint Planner on a screen or perhaps a whiteboard.

▲ Encourage the team to be bold and kind, yet rigorous when helping each other improve their skills and their message maps. You, of course, need to strike a balance. I raise this because I see a lot of teams holding back in fear of upsetting colleagues, which is a missed opportunity for everyone. It may help to explicitly encourage everyone to give and receive suggestions from others.

Extend the team's learning into the coming week

Here are some ways to extend learning:

▲ Set homework to further explore structures and how to assess the quality of thinking inside your message map. This week's homework is substantive, focusing on structure and synthesis. Set the following, using your chosen resource:

1. *Engage* – read chapter 5 on ideas for firming up your messaging using first principles and the SCORE framework.
2. *Engage* course – complete the modules on the same topics.

▲ Ask each person to build a message map the following week. They might do it in pairs or threes.

Collaboration is key to stimulating greater learning. Different people notice different things and together they go further. It also establishes productive habits going forward where they can review each other's structures before sending to you for your own input.

I suggest keeping the groups to two or three people to ensure all are actively involved. Once groups grow in size, some participants sit back and let others do the work (and get the benefit).

Week 3: Firm up your messaging using first principles

As you can see, we are layering into the process from more general ideas before getting into the specifics. This session will be the most intense of all, so I encourage you to roll your sleeves up and dive in. You may also like to allow for a longer session to accommodate the level of challenge.

We will focus on mastering the structured thinking principles that underpin message maps and are central to squeezing out the maximum quality insights from your information.

As with last week, first help recap the topics covered, seed the questions, offer a challenge and then set expectations.

Reflect on the past week and recap on first principles

Hopefully now you are three sessions in, you have great examples from the team. Be sure to call these out because it's easy to start taking it for granted, even though the team may still be grappling with how to apply the ideas well.

This week's focus is on structuring your message. Here's a sample script for your recap:

By now you will have realised that the techniques we are using are a thinking tool, not just a communication tool.

This week we will dive more deeply into the structured thinking aspects of this work, so we can iterate effectively on our messaging.

We will make sure the three key elements of a structure work. It means having a short introduction with a clear 'what' and 'why', followed by one insightful message that ties the whole story together.

This main message is then supported one of two ways: with a grouped set of ideas or a deductive chain.

Today we'll make sure we all become comfortable with how each of the elements functions.

Ask questions to stimulate discussion

This week, ask your team the following:

▲ Have you collaborated with someone else to think through the strategy or structure of a message map yet?

▲ Have you used the SCORE framework yet? How did it go? (summary below and in the PowerPoint Planner for quick reference).

▲ Can you share an example with everyone, or the person sitting next to you? What worked? What didn't?

SCORE framework summary

Challenge the team by building message maps together

Given the importance of getting the links between ideas within a message map right, I encourage you to focus closely on structural accuracy during this conversation. Here are a couple of ideas:

▲ Allow 15 minutes to together Scan and Score a message map for something relevant tot he team. Recap the approach and then split the group into pairs or threes and ask them to do a speed review of a message map of their own or one you bring forward. You might ask them to each offer one positive and one area for improvement.

▲ Regroup and allow a further 30 minutes to discuss the SCORE for as many of the message maps as you can. Ask groups to share and explain their scoring and to test it with others in the room.

I suggest curating the examples and doing your own review before the session to help you extract maximum value from these conversations.

Extend the team's learning into the coming week

Use the following to extend learning:

▲ Set homework to cover the remainder of all learning resources, including how to talk through a message map, present the message map in prose format and as a PowerPoint presentation. Set the following:
  1. *Engage* – read chapter 6 on techniques for finalising their documents. Ask your team to also read chapters 7 and 8 to set them up to flourish into the longer term to complete the series.
  2. *Engage* course – complete all remaining modules.

▲ Encourage your team to experiment with message maps in their routine work and take special note when someone 'gives it a go'. Deductive structures are typically harder to employ, but worth the effort.

▲ Continue to focus on effort rather than perfection, because it may take some time for the group to become confident at structuring message maps.

▲ Start requiring all draft papers to come to you as a message map accompanied by the strategy page. This will show that you are taking the process seriously. Now is a good time for message mapping to start becoming 'the done thing'.

Week 4: Finalising your document

At this stage, your team can start turning message maps into actual papers or presentations.

Sometimes the message map itself will be the 'artifact' and your team won't need to create anything else. This can be the case when preparing for a meeting and you use the map as speaking notes or when socialising messaging with key stakeholders who then offer their support without a need for a more formal discussion.

Mostly, however, your team will need to turn the message map into a formal communication once you've landed the messaging together.

Reflect on the past week and recap documents

This is another good opportunity to share your own reflections of what you are seeing from the team. Do you have any good ideas to share? Has anyone prepared a paper or presentation that has demonstrably used the ideas? Could you see how the thinking in the message map drove the document structure?

To recap this week's focus, remind your team that the key to turning a message map into a paper, PowerPoint or another deliverable is to match the messaging hierarchy with the formatting hierarchy within the document.

This means they should include a short executive summary that includes a brief 'what' and 'why', followed by a highly visible main message that is then supported by two to five supporting points. These supporting points are organised as either a grouping or deductive structure.

You team may be tempted to tweak the message map and add further ideas into the structure at this stage. Both of these things are a natural consequence of thinking further about the topic and are fine, with one caveat: any additions must have a logical home within the structure. If they are 'backup', they can instead be added to an appendix.

Ask questions to stimulate discussion

Here are some questions for this week:

- ▲ How has your message mapping experience been this week?
- ▲ What challenges have you experienced when flipping your message map into a deliverable of some kind?
- ▲ What templates do we need to adjust to accommodate message maps?
- ▲ Where can we use the whole message map as a section within a template?
- ▲ Where do we need to 'slice and dice' the message map across different sections of a template?

You may find my video that discusses 'hacking' templates to accommodate message maps useful at this stage, if you have not yet accessed it. (This video is available in the Clarity Hub Leaders' Toolkit.)

Challenge the team to flip message maps into documents together

Ask the team to bring some message maps and documents to this session that everyone can work on together as follows:

▲ Allow 30 minutes to work in small groups to review the prose and PowerPoint samples I've provided in *Engage* (chapter 6). Compare these to recent papers and presentations the team has prepared and discuss opportunities for improvement.

▲ Allow a further 30-plus minutes to flip a message map for a commonly prepared document into the final communication version, either in small groups or as a whole. Allow time after the discussion to finesse the message map and add to a sample library.

Extend the team's learning into the coming week

This coming week is a great time to fine-tune any annotations on templates to help the team align message mapping principles with your existing corporate templates.

It is also time to be on the lookout for backsliding. If someone sends you a paper to review without having provided you with a message map first, reject it. You will only need to do it once and the team will get the message.

In the next chapter, I offer ideas to help teams, to embed the approach into their regular ways of working.

In the meantime I will explain how you might run a workshop as an alternative way to introduce the approach.

Facilitate a short, practical workshop

In this section, I help you build your team's skills via a short and impactful workshop. You can choose whether you develop your own workshop materials or acquire my Workshop Kit, based on what I currently offer my clients.

I suggest having a quick pre-meeting, followed by a workshop and then coaching the team to embed the habits over time.

Here I describe how I run the sessions. I weave live work in with engaging practical exercises, mixing in breakouts for the team to prepare sections of live communication. You can decide whether to teach concepts from the beginning, or to reinforce concepts the team has learned from reading *Engage* or completing the online course.

Wherever possible, I ask my clients to learn the basics before we work together. This means that during the workshop we can reinforce concepts, challenge ideas and dig deeply into using them. In your case, this will make it faster and easier to facilitate too.

Below I explain how to run a quick preparation call to set your team up for success and share the key slides you will need. I'll then offer a plan for the 3-hour team workshop.

Prep Call: Introduce approach and provide pre-work

I have designed this to be practical so the team builds communication along with you rather than listens to you discuss the theory.

With a modicum of guidance, the team will be able to practise using the techniques on live work. This makes the most of the time spent together while also bringing the approach to life.

Before you facilitate the workshop, however, the team needs to be prepared. They need to understand the following:

- why this matters
- what they will learn (the two slides to the right may help with this)
- what is expected of them
- when to finish any pre-work
- what to bring to the workshop.

Allow up to 30 minutes for this call so you don't rush and set everyone up well.

Here are the key slides for that call as reference before I guide you through the workshop itself.

I have animated the downloadable versions so it is easy for you to work through the approach step by step.

I think you will know where to find them in PowerPoint form by now! They are available in the Clarity Hub Leaders' Toolkit.

Prep Call slides

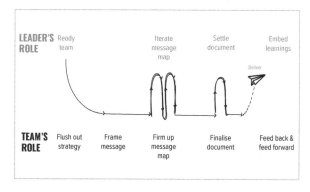

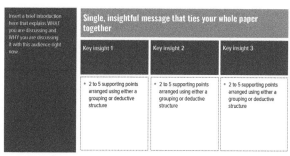

Workshop schedule

LEARN	DO	PURPOSE	ACTIVITY	TIMER
10		Familiarise all with the plan	Welcome and introduce the session	0
10		Focus everyone on approach	Before and after exercise	10
5	15	Develop communication strategy	Appreciate that you must take time to think through your engagement strategy before drafting your message	20
5	15	Structure the introduction	Clarify the question they want to set the audience up to ask	40
5	5	Synthesise main message	Articulate the main message in a sentence	1 hr
15		Structure supporting ideas	Familiarise with both grouping and deductive structures, focus on groupings	1 hr 10
	10	**BIO BREAK**		**1 hr 20**
	30	Build out supporting structure for message map, iterate to improve	Apply the ideas, consolidating by building a real example	1 hr 50
5	15	Review message map using SCORE framework	Consolidate concepts, reaffirm the value of collaborating to get to a better story sooner	2 hr 10
5		Learn to telegraph the hierarchy of the messaging	Close the conceptual loop between the message map and the document	2 hr 15
	15	Convert message map into a paper or presentation	Practice linking a message map to a real communication	2 hr 30
	15	Next steps and debrief	Make it stick!	2 hr 45

Workshop: Work through message mapping from beginning to end

My goal when running these workshops is to break the learning into interactive chunks.

At each key stage I pause and ask the group to apply the ideas to a simple, live communication of their own.

I find emails are great for this as they are usually simple enough that the team can focus on applying the concepts rather than getting lost in the detail. I suggest using an email of five or more lines, but not more than half a page. A simple, routine paper may also work well.

I will now step out each of the elements for you.

DESIRED OUTCOMES

- Team knows how to use a message map to think through a piece of communication using a grouping structure.
- Team understands the basics around deductive structures.
- Team is familiar with the tools for structuring their messaging.
- Team understands the importance of nailing the messaging for their communication before preparing it.

NECESSARY TOOLS

- Workshop presentation and handout, which will include key PowerPoint Planner slides
- SCORE framework for checking the quality of the thinking
- Before and after exercises to draw out common challenges and mistakes. Use examples and solutions of your own design or pre-prepared and tested versions from my Workshop Kit

WORKSHOP SCHEDULE

I have included a time-stamped planner for you to the left as a guide.

Discuss differences between a before and after example

Offer a 'before' example and ask group to review it with the principles in mind:

- Can they see the messaging at a glance?
- What is the main message?
- How hard does the audience need to work to understand it?

Offer a reworked version of the same story that you are proud of, so they can see how a story evolves. Ask the following:

- What similarities and differences do they notice between the two?
- Can they see the main message easily?

- Can they find the top-level logic at a glance?

Explain how to think through communication strategy

Use the strategy page from the PowerPoint Planner (thumbnail below) as your guide.

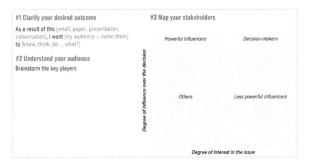

Work through the strategy for a live example either as a whole group or in small breakouts, then debrief. Ask them what is different about this approach and the way they normally think about our purpose and audiences?

Explain how to draw the audience in with the introduction and main message

Introduce the key elements of the introduction: the what, why and audience question which together draw your audience toward your main message.

Offer strong and weak examples to illustrate how introductions can flow, while hiding the question.

Ask participants to work out what question they naturally want to ask after the what and why. It helps to have a poor one that

does not enable them to guess the question and then a better one for comparison.

Explain that these two elements draw the audience toward their one main message.

Explain key criteria for a main message: it needs to be insightful, overarching and short at 25 words or less.

If time, send them back to their groups for 15 minutes to draft the introduction and main message for their communication or hold until after supporting points.

Explain how to structure the supporting points as either a grouping or deductive structure

Here are two slides to guide this discussion.

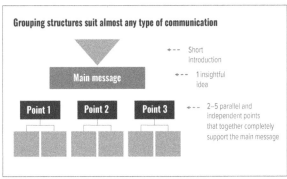

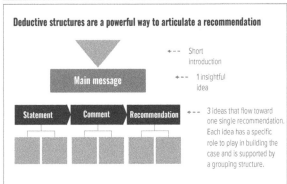

Explain how grouping and deductive structures are both similar and different.

- BIO BREAK - 10 MINUTES -

Recap and send everyone to their groups for 30 minutes to draft their message maps (or do together as a whole group)

Regroup and explain they can use the Pattern Picker framework to help them identify which structure will suit their situation best. Here is a skeleton. The full details are included in the appendix.

1 – CLARIFY	2 – REVIEW		3 – FIND		4 – FRAME
I need my audience to ...	To achieve that I must explain ...		... then pick a pattern		... and structure it
> Action > Implement > Support	Action plans	xxxx	Nike	**XXXX**	xxxx
> Know > Understand	Findings	xxxx	Nugget	**XXXX**	xxxx
> Trust	Updates	xxxx	All is Well	**XXXX**	xxxx
> Agree > Approve > Change > Decide > Endorse	Strategies	xxxx	Golden	**XXXX**	xxxx
		xxxx	Make the Case	**XXXX**	xxxx
		xxxx	Oh Dear	**XXXX**	xxxx
	Options	xxxx	Short List	**XXXX**	xxxx
		xxxx	This or That	**XXXX**	xxxx
	Improvements	xxxx	Change Tack	**XXXX**	xxxx
		xxxx	Top up	**XXXX**	xxxx

Send them to their groups for 30 minutes to prepare their draft structure. Visit the groups to offer suggestions.

Talk through one of the group's example together, using the SCORE framework as a reference for improvement ideas (see summary to the top right).

I suggest keeping the detailed framework close for reference.

SCORE framework summary

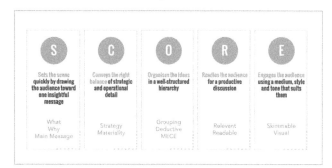

Explain how a message map links to a document

Illustrate with an example, eg 105 reports story, as both a paper and a presentation. Explain that the principles are the same regardless of format: a short introduction followed by a skimmable story stepped out message by message.

Gather takeaways

I ask each participant for one key thing they have learned and then ask them to choose who goes next. This is a beautiful way to get them to reinforce what they have learned and to teach each other.

Set go-forward expectations

Explain that you want a draft message map with the strategy page for every major communication going forward before the paper or presentation is prepared.

Ask the team to peer review drafts before they come to you also.

After the workshop you will want to reinforce what you have done together by working on live communication.

Working closely with the team to think through papers and presentations at this early stage is the most natural way to do this. You will over time step back as they become more independent, but for now rolling your sleeves up for live projects will help you all.

I recommend locking in coaching sessions within a week after the workshop if at all possible. This proximity will help the ideas stick for all of you.

These sessions will ideally fit within your natural communication cadence to focus on a relevant and current paper or presentation.

When I facilitate these, I rely on the PowerPoint planner to guide the process. This is a painless way to remember to incorporate all of the message mapping steps.

Now that you have built your team's skills, let's look at ways to help you and the team flourish into the long term.

CHAPTER 9

Flourish into the long term

A common idea in learning and development is that 10 per cent of the benefit comes from course work and training, 20 per cent comes from coaching, and 70 per cent comes from challenging assignments that have direct relevance to someone's role.[1] This means that much of the real learning happens over time and on the job. It also reaffirms why your role as leader is so central to improving the quality of papers and presentations that your team delivers.

The following comment from Kathy, a learning and development specialist, reinforces this view:

I've seen very ordinary programs make a big difference because they were embedded well. The embedding is essential and must be driven by the leaders.

This sums up why I've written this book. I can only help you so far. Most of the work is up to you in the near and longer term.

So, having helped your team build their skills and adjust their operating rhythm, I now offer ideas to help you all flourish into the longer term.

I've broken the timeline into two sections:

▲ The first three months to fine-tune skills and behaviours
▲ Thereafter for making the new ways of working 'stick'.

---

1 Michael Lombardo and Robert Eichinger expressed the rationale behind this 70:20:10 model in *The Career Architect Development Planner.*

▲ First three months: Fine-tune skills and behaviours

Now that your team is familiar with message mapping, it's time to fine-tune skills and behaviours.

You want them to go beyond 'knowing a few good ideas' to being really good at structuring their thinking so they can consistently clarify and convey high quality ideas.

This will require materials to remove barriers and prompt behaviours, measurement to identify wins and areas for further focus, and motivation to keep everyone moving forward as the novelty wanes. I unpack each of these here.

Materials to remove barriers and prompt behaviours

This is the time to both make message mapping as easy as possible and reduce any excuses the team may have for not following through. Here are two key ideas to help:

▲ Consider setting up email signatures that follow the format. Emails of five lines or more offer an easy opportunity for practising the thinking strategies that underpin message mapping. I include two example templates in the

appendix, and provide 'cut and paste' versions in the Clarity Hub Toolkit.

▲ Build a folder, SharePoint page or similar resource hub to house sample documents from the team's work, links to tools offered in this book, templates and other resources.

▲ Tailor remaining templates to accommodate message maps. I suggest adding message mapping instructions into the templates to help the team connect the dots between a message map and the template. It will help the team, for example, to know where to add the introduction, main message and supporting points within the prescribed template format. This seems simple, but can be a big barrier for people attempting to use the ideas while also complying with corporate conventions.

Measure to identify wins and areas for further focus

Like with any project, the only way to know if you are achieving your goals is to measure your progress. In this section, I run through several light-touch strategies to help you do that.

Agree effort and quality milestones and revisit them regularly

Use effort milestones to be confident the team continues to use the approach regularly. Ensure the following:

- ▲ You brief the team as early as you can for every paper going to a project steering committee, the senior leadership team or the board.
- ▲ The team always peer reviews message map drafts before they are sent to you.
- ▲ You as leader received a draft message map to review for all papers going to key decision-making bodies over the period.
- ▲ Everyone structures emails of five lines or more, with a short introduction, a visible main message and a well-organised set of supporting points.
- ▲ Team members are using message maps to think through substantial contributions to meetings.

Use quality milestones to demonstrate that the effort is paying off. For example:

- ▲ One-page message maps progressively earn higher SCORES when you and your colleagues review them.
- ▲ Emails are of increasing quality and so leading to shorter 'chains', faster responses and less 'firefighting'.

- ▲ Stakeholders are making more comments about the quality of communication received from your team.

You might even set yourselves a challenge of receiving a compliment from a particularly surly stakeholder!

Ask the team to self-evaluate their progress and debrief regularly with peers

You might do this self-evaluation and debriefing fortnightly for the first month or two, and then monthly after that to maintain focus and calibrate progress.

Honesty combined with psychological safety will be key here. This requires you to give permission for real life to intervene, rather than focusing primarily on 'perfection'.

This does not mean you should avoid aiming high, but if the team is not comfortable admitting they are finding message mapping difficult, or have been avoiding using the technique, they may pretend all is well even when they know it is not.

You can lead by admitting when you could have done better – for example, by providing better or earlier briefs, or holding people more to account for providing one-page message maps for you to review.

You can also reinforce the importance of effort over results in the early stage of learning something new. The more you all use the techniques, the better you will get.

Keep track of the amount of time you spend reworking team papers and why

Ask yourself the following questions:

- ▲ Am I continuing to reduce the amount of time I spend reviewing or rewriting the team's papers?
- ▲ What caused me to rewrite a paper? Is this a one-off or systemic problem? If systemic, what can I do to further fine-tune our process to avoid a repeat?

Motivate to keep the team moving forward as novelty wanes

This is an area that is easy to ignore. You have offered the team an opportunity to build their capability and will continue to coach them going forward. You also need to bridge the gap between initial excitement and seeing message mapping embedded into day-to-day work.

Maintaining motivation will be central to successfully baking message mapping into your operating rhythm. Here are four ideas to help.

Celebrate successes both within your team and with stakeholders

I think this is such an easy win, but one that leaders tell me they often forget to do. So, here are some quick ideas:

- ▲ Compliment team members personally when you see them using the approach in emails. This can be as simple as a quick PS at the bottom of your reply.
- ▲ Forward great examples to the team for broader recognition, explaining what you appreciated about this particular example.
- ▲ Let the team know when a stakeholder makes a comment about the improved clarity of papers they receive.

Hold awards ceremonies

My colleague Mike Sherman did this to great effect when global director for knowledge management and insights at Synovate in Singapore. Here is what he shared with me:

In my last year at Synovate, I spent a quarter of my time in the London office. Every quarter each team had to submit at least one report for the reporting award.

I read the reports and chose three winners and three notable mentions.

I then explained what the winners had done to win – it generated a lot of excitement and pride and helped me underline key concepts in a very collegial manner.

Hold regular ShowCases

For those not familiar with Agile ways of working, ShowCases are an opportunity for the team to share what they have been working on over the past period. Preparing for a five-minute presentation is a practical and bite-sized opportunity to practise while achieving a useful team outcome.

You can ask the team to prepare a one-page executive summary based on a message map with a couple of supporting slides if needed. Equally, you could ask the team to provide feedback to each other: one strength and one opportunity for improvement for everyone.

Mandate the use of message maps in preparing for performance reviews

Performance reviews happen regularly in every organisation and so are a natural opportunity for practice at a time when team members are motivated to handle the meeting well. Asking your team to prepare a message map for their review will help team members not only think through their situation but also clarify

their own perspective on their past performance and future ambitions.

This will give you a number of regular opportunities to consolidate the team's capability before baking message mapping into your team's day-to-day operating rhythm.

Don't let the team 'tweak' the structure

As I was about to put this book to bed, I saw a beautiful example of what not to do. The team was using their one-pager to brief an executive, but couldn't quite land the main message.

So, the fix was to remove the main message from the one-pager altogether!

It took me a minute to work out what was wrong as the formatting was neat and all the other elements were in place.

This is a great example of the difference between a message map and a template. A template has topics for discussion, which if not relevant, can be easily removed.

A message map is different. It is a framework for clarifying your thinking which requires all elements to be in place.

▲ Thereafter: Make the new ways of working 'stick'

By now the core operating rhythm will be humming and your team will have made significant improvements to the clarity and quality of their communication. You should also be seeing a significant lift in velocity as the team prepares better documents more quickly that support better, faster decision-making.

This is fantastic but also a risk because you and the team may start to backslide as the novelty wears off, new team members join and new projects come into focus.

Here are five ideas to help you all keep on track.

Conduct regular pulse checks

Adding a pulse check into the agenda for the first team meeting of each month is quick and easy to do. Use the following questions:

▲ What are we seeing more of?
  - Message mapping language embedded in our day-to-day discussions?
  - Team members routinely offering rigorous feedback on message maps?
  - Decisions being made quickly on the back of team communication?

▲ What are we seeing less of?
  - Leaders reworking team papers?
  - Leadership forums rejecting papers that contain good ideas?
  - 'Firefighting' stemming from poor communication?
  - Lengthy and confusing email chains?

Set up a champions rota

I suggest rotating the champion role across the team for defined three- to six-month stints. This reduces the risk of members of the team abdicating their own role as a communicator to one potentially highly skilled team member. It also increases the chance of fresh ideas being deployed. Champions would be responsible for delivering the agreed 'make it stick' activities over a set period, keeping you in regular touch with activities and progress.

Update collateral

Organisations routinely update templates and ways of working. Make sure to update key templates with message mapping prompts to bake message mapping into new ways of working.

Simple barriers like this can hamper the team's best efforts. So removing them is important.

Refresh the learning

Message mapping is a skill that develops over time, with challenges emerging every time new stakeholders arrive, new roles are undertaken and new team members join. You might find it useful to refresh the learning at regular intervals. Here are two techniques to try:

▲ Ask the team to read a chapter from *Engage* or watch one of the online modules again and bring a takeaway to share with the group.

▲ Find the detailed questions from the SCORE framework to be a useful guide in adding to their comments or creating a quiz. I have laid it out in the appendix as reference and for easy finding.

Continue celebrating!

It is so easy to move onto the next thing, which of course you will. But when you do so, keep message mapping on the radar so you and the team don't fall back into old habits.

Make it a habit to compliment people who make a great effort and those who achieve high scores. Create formal celebrations, too, such as quarterly awards for most improved and for great message maps, and when notable compliments are received from senior leaders.

If you lock in simple but regular celebrations, message mapping will embed itself as a natural part of your operating rhythm despite distractions. New leaders who are unfamiliar won't change your approach. Crazy busy periods won't derail you. Nor will a high level of staff turnover.

New team members will quickly realise this is 'the way you do things' and get on board, and new leaders will appreciate the clarity and insight found within your team's communication.

CHAPTER 10

Start now

I hope I have persuaded you that you no longer need to routinely work late at night and into weekends to rework your team's papers.

In fact, I hope I have gone further than that. I hope you have already started using the ideas and thought about how to introduce the ideas to your team.

If you haven't, start now! Download the PowerPoint Planner[1] and work through the process for a communication of your own.

- ▲ 'Strategise' so you are confident you are communicating the right message to the right people.
- ▲ 'Synthesise' your ideas into a message map so you are crystal clear about the messages you need to convey.
- ▲ 'Visualise' your message in whatever format you need, being sure to offer a clear and compelling hierarchy of easily digestible ideas.

Then, decide how to build your team's skills. Whatever capability-building path you take, engage your team by lifting your communication process and standards.

Remember to:

- ▲ Ready the team to ensure they know what's required.
- ▲ Iterate their message maps to nail the messaging.
- ▲ Settle the document using structure to guide the review.
- ▲ Embed the learning to create a positive flywheel effect.

Do you want to cut the number of times you need to review your team's papers in half? Get faster approvals for key decisions? Improve team morale? Get more done? *And* lead a high-performing team that delivers maximum value?

Getting these kinds of results might mean stepping outside your own comfort zone and enabling your team to do their jobs fully so you can step into the strategy zone yourself.

Whatever your motivation, it is my fervent hope that you and your team enjoy the fruits of greater clarity of messaging, quality of insights and velocity of progress *today*.

---

1   ClarityFirstProgram.com/ClarityHub

APPENDIX

Appendix

▲ Core toolkit

▲ Leaders' toolkit

▲ References and further reading

Elevate message mapping framework

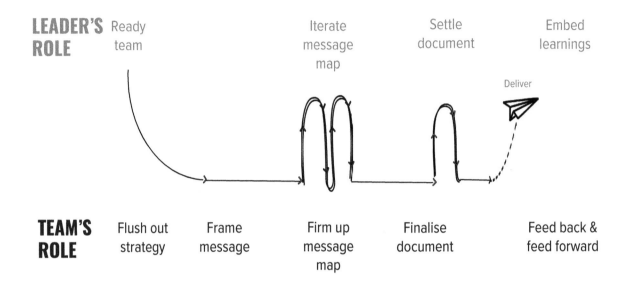

LEADER'S ROLE

Ready team — Iterate message map — Settle document — Embed learnings

Deliver

TEAM'S ROLE

Flush out strategy — Frame message — Firm up message map — Finalise document — Feed back & feed forward

Stakeholder analysis templates

#1 Clarify your desired outcome

As a result of this [email, paper, presentation, conversation], **I want** [my audience – name them] **to** [know, think, do ... what?]

#2 Understand your audience

Brainstorm the key players

#3 Map your stakeholders

Degree of influence over the decision

Powerful influencers	*Decision-makers*
Others	*Less powerful influencers*

Develop stakeholder strategy if key decision makers are objectors

UNDERSTAND & SHIFT		What do they think now?	What do you want them to think?
	Objectors	Why don't they understand or agree?	
	Neutral	Why aren't they fully supportive?	

LEVERAGE		What do they support?	How much will they invest?	How could they help 'convert' your objectors?
	Champions	You? The concept? The goal?	Time? Money or other resources? Influence? Relationships?	Explain why they should support your idea?
				Ask them to meet so you can explain?
				Offer them a trade?
	Advocates			Help you revise your concept to make it more acceptable?
				Something else?

Pattern Picker framework

1 – CLARIFY OUTCOME	2 – REVIEW POTENTIAL MESSAGES	3 – FIND MESSAGE		4 – FRAME MESSAGE
I need my audience to ...	**To achieve that I must explain ...**	**... then pick a pattern**		**... and structure it**
> Action > Endorse > Implement > Support	Action plans How to proceed	Nike	**Do X to fix Y**	2 to 5 steps ordered by sequence or scale
> Know > Understand	Findings What analysis revealed	Nugget	**We found X**	2 to 5 points of evidence ordered by scale of importance
> Have confidence > Trust	Updates The status is green, project is going well	All is Well	**We are in good shape**	2 to 5 reasons why we are in good shape, ordered by task or time
> Agree > Approve > Change > Decide > Endorse	Strategies How to capture a new opportunity	Golden	**Do X to capture opportunity A**	Opportunity A is attractive, X will capture it, so do X
	How to solve a problem or capture an opportunity	Make the Case	**Doing X will fix Y**	2 to 5 reasons explaining why X is the right way to fix Y
	How to solve a problem that is new to your audience	Oh Dear	**Do X to solve problem Y**	Problem Y matters, but X will fix it, so do X
	Options Which options to evaluate	Short List	**Consider these for solving Y**	2 to 5 reasons to consider these options
	Best way to capture an opportunity or solve a problem	This or That	**Option X offers best approach**	We explored these options for solving Y, but option X is best, so implement X
	Improvements How to address an emerging opportunity or risk	Change Tack	**Make a change to reach goal**	Have made progress, but need to make a change to reach goal, so make a change
	How to succeed when you meet only some necessary criteria	Top up	**Top up to succeed at Y**	Succeeding at Y requires X, but we have only some of X in place, so top up

Grouping Structure Summary

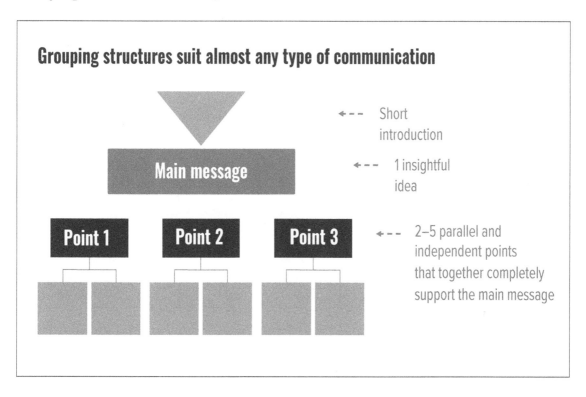

Grouping structure with details

A short introduction that explains WHAT you are discussing. It should include information that is familiar to the audience and bring their minds to a recent relevant event or issue.

Most likely a single sentence that explains WHY you want to discuss the topic outlined above with your audience now.

The question you want to answer, which your audience will naturally want to ask after they have heard or read what you are discussing and why.

One single insightful message that is 25 words or less and summarises or ideally synthesises your whole story.

The single question your audience will naturally want to ask after learning your main message. This is unlikely to be written into your final document but helps power your thinking.

Point 1: The first of 2 to 5 points that respond to the same question your audience will naturally ask after hearing or reading the main message.	Point 2: The second of 2 to 5 points that responds to the same question the audience will naturally ask after hearing or reading the main message.	Points 3 to 5: More 'parallel' points if needed to further support the main message.
• The first of 2 to 5 sub-points that form either a grouping or deductive structure to elaborate on the top-line point. • The second sub-point that follows the first, adopting either a grouping or deductive structure. • The third and subsequent sub-points, if necessary.	• As for point 1	• As for point 1

Deductive structure summary

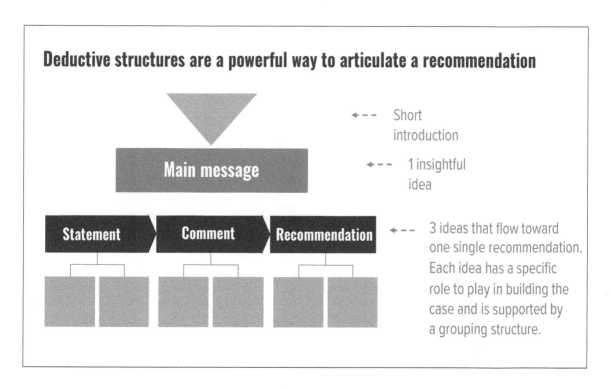

Deductive structures are a powerful way to articulate a recommendation

Main message

Statement → Comment → Recommendation

← - - Short introduction

← - - 1 insightful idea

← - - 3 ideas that flow toward one single recommendation. Each idea has a specific role to play in building the case and is supported by a grouping structure.

Deductive structure with details

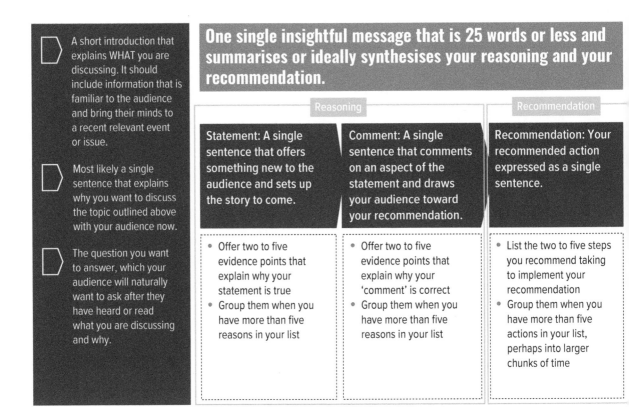

A short introduction that explains WHAT you are discussing. It should include information that is familiar to the audience and bring their minds to a recent relevant event or issue.

Most likely a single sentence that explains why you want to discuss the topic outlined above with your audience now.

The question you want to answer, which your audience will naturally want to ask after they have heard or read what you are discussing and why.

One single insightful message that is 25 words or less and summarises or ideally synthesises your reasoning and your recommendation.

Reasoning

Recommendation

Statement: A single sentence that offers something new to the audience and sets up the story to come.

Comment: A single sentence that comments on an aspect of the statement and draws your audience toward your recommendation.

Recommendation: Your recommended action expressed as a single sentence.

- Offer two to five evidence points that explain why your statement is true
- Group them when you have more than five reasons in your list

- Offer two to five evidence points that explain why your 'comment' is correct
- Group them when you have more than five reasons in your list

- List the two to five steps you recommend taking to implement your recommendation
- Group them when you have more than five actions in your list, perhaps into larger chunks of time

SCORE framework summary

Sets the scene **quickly by drawing the audience toward one insightful message**	Conveys the right balance **of strategic and operational detail**	Organises the ideas **in a well-structured hierarchy**	Readies the audience **for a productive discussion**	Engages the audience **using a medium, style and tone that suits them**
What Why Main Message	Strategy Materiality	Grouping Deductive MECE	Relevant Readable	Skimmable Visual

SCORE framework - detailed

I ask whether the communication does the following Does it …

S – Set the scene quickly by drawing the audience toward one insightful message by …

1. *Explaining **WHAT** is being discussed early:*
   a. Quickly reminding the audience about the familiar problem, opportunity or observation the paper will discuss
   b. Introducing that topic in a way that is timely and tight
2. *Explaining **WHY** this topic is being discussed now*
3. *Offering **one insightful and visible main message** that unifies the whole paper in 25 words or less.*

C – Convey the right balance of strategic and operational detail by …

4. *Positioning the story appropriately in relation to strategy*
5. *Aligning with the right materiality thresholds for this audience*

O – Organise the ideas in a well-structured hierarchy by …

6. *Aligning ideas at every level of a grouping structure four ways:*
   a. Number: Each group has two to five ideas
   b. Type: Each idea is the same kind of idea as its peers
   c. Vertically: Each idea answers the single natural question prompted by the idea above
   d. Horizontally: Ideas are arranged logically, likely by sequence or scale
7. *Ensuring the top-line ideas in a deductive structure each play their specific role, i.e.*
   a. The statement anchors the narrative around one substantive idea that is both new to the audience and broader in scope than the comment
   b. The comment narrows the discussion to focus on one key concept that was introduced in the statement
   c. The statement and comment are so persuasive that together they prepare your audience for your recommendation, so it does not come as a surprise

8. *Supporting the top-line of a deductive structure well, which means that:*

   a. Both the statement and comment are supported by tightly grouped ideas

   b. The recommendation ('therefore') is supported by tightly grouped actions

9. Avoiding gaps and overlaps, i.e. the ideas are MECE (Mutually Exclusive, Collectively Exhaustive). This involves:

   - Categorising and labeling ideas correctly

   - Avoiding ideas overlapping each other

   - Leaving nothing out

R – Readies the audience for a productive discussion by ...

10. *Focusing only on matters relevant to the desired outcome*

11. *Being easily readable, using language that is active and parallel throughout, i.e. by:*

    a. Synthesising or summarising ideas at every level into fully formed sentences that the audience will find insightful, i.e. they are useful, impactful and interesting

    b. Expressing ideas clearly, so the audience doesn't need to ask for clarification

    c. Using parallel language so the ideas obviously match each other

E – Engages the audience using a medium, style and tone that suits them by ...

12. *Formatting ideas so it is easy to skim the hierarchy of the messaging, in any medium*

13. *Using simple images, charts and diagrams to help the audience quickly grasp ideas*

Example message map

Meeting regulatory requirements requires us to transition all 105 legacy reports into the case system by the end of this financial year. We have now reviewed the associated work plans and received updated estimates.

We are now ready to share those estimates with you along with potential ways forward.

What are you suggesting?

Delivering the 105 reports means either investing $1.2m to $2m more over the coming two years or renegotiating requirements with the regulator.

Despite stress testing all budgets, we can't transition all 105 regulatory reports within the agreed $2m budget this financial year.	This means we need to make trade-offs when finalising the project workplans.	Therefore, we ask you to advise which tradeoffs we can make.
Updated estimates for database came back at $2m, which is 2.5 x the original budget due to more comprehensive scoping. **Budgets for other aspects of the work have not materially changed.** • Workflow remains same. • API linking ditto. • Operational teams ditto. **Work required for reports identified since June last year has not been factored in.**	**We could meet the scope by spending $1.2m to $2m more over the coming two years.** • We could deliver everything in FY23 with $1.2m more during FY23, or • We could deliver some in FY23, some in FY24 with $2m or more in total. **We could renegotiate scope or time with the regulator.** • We could limit the scope and deliver only the top 70 reports by FY23 (fix existing 36, do another 35ish) within the current budget, or • We could seek agreement from the regulator to further extend the project and deliver all at a later date.	**Decide whether to spend more ...** • Decide whether to increase funding by $1.2m for FY23. • Decide whether to budget $2m more for the project in total and roll into next year. **Decide whether to renegotiate ...** • Decide whether to pitch the regulator to accept the top 70 reports as adequate for FY23. • Decide whether to seek extensions.

The Regulatory Projects Steering Committee advises which trade-offs the team can make to finalise workplans for 2024.

EXECUTIVE SUMMARY

Meeting regulatory requirements requires us to transition all 105 legacy reports into the case system by the end of this financial year. We have now reviewed the plans and estimates and are ready to discuss potential ways forward.

In sum, we need to decide to either spend an extra $1.2 million to $2 million over the coming two years or renegotiate requirements with the regulator. Here is an outline of our high-level position before going into more detail below.

1. Despite stress testing all budgets, we can't transition all 105 regulatory reports within the agreed $2 million budget this financial year.
2. This means we need to make trade-offs when finalising the workplans.
3. As a result, we ask you to advise which trade-offs we can make.

DISCUSSION

Despite stress testing all budgets, we can't transition all 105 regulatory reports within the agreed $2 million budget this financial year. After conducting the thorough review that you requested, we found

- Updated estimates for database came back at $2 million – 2.5 times the original budget due to a more comprehensive scoping. (See appendix for breakdown.)
- Budgets for other aspects of the work have not materially changed. Costs for workflow, API linking, and operational aspects remain steady.
- Any reports that have been identified as needing to be reworked since June last year have not been factored into this.

This means we need to make trade-offs when finalising the workplans. Given these trade-offs require your endorsement to be implemented, we offer alternatives for your consideration.

Option 1: Spend $1.2 million more now or $2 million more later. We could then deliver either

- everything in FY23 with $1.2 million more during FY23
- some in FY23, some in FY24 with $2 million or more.

Option 2: Renegotiate scope or time with the regulator. If taking this path, we could

- limit the scope to delivering only the top 70 reports by FY23 within the current budget and negotiate with the regulator to accept this as final, or
- seek agreement from the regulator to further extend project timelines.

As a result, we ask you to advise which trade-offs we can make. This involves deciding whether to

- Spend more by either
  - increasing funding by $1.2 million for FY23, or
  - budgeting $2 million more for the project in total and roll into next year.
- Renegotiate by either
  - accepting the top 70 reports in FY23 as adequate and convincing the regulator to agree, or
  - seeking extensions from the regulator.

We understand this is not the outcome you were hoping for but look forward to your decision as to the best way forward.

ATTACHMENTS

Detailed financial breakdown of the updated financial estimates for all aspects of the 105 reports project.

SUBMITTED BY

Ryan Bloggs, Program Manager, Regulatory Projects

Title page explains why we are presenting re: the legacy reports

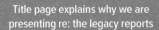

R&S BANK

LEGACY REPORT PROGRAM – CRITICAL DECISION POINT RE: PATH FORWARD FOR 105 REPORTS

PROGRAM STEERCO
JULY, 2023

Background page offers the what and why (hide when presenting)

Meeting regulatory requirements requires us to transition all 105 legacy reports into the case system by the end of this financial year.

We have now reviewed plans and estimates and are ready to discuss potential ways forward.

Executive summary offers high level message + navigation aid

We need to decide to either spend $1.2 million to $2 million more over the coming two years or to renegotiate requirements with the regulator

01 Despite stress-testing all budgets, we can't transition all 105 regulatory reports within the agreed $2 million budget this financial year.

02 This means we need to decide which trade-offs to make as we rescope the project.

03 Therefore, we ask you to advise which trade-offs we can make in rescoping the project.

Navigator in top right corner of each page

Despite stress-testing all budgets, we can't transition all 105 regulatory reports within the agreed $2 million budget this financial year

 01 Updated estimates for database came back at $2m, which is 2.5 x the original budget due to more comprehensive scoping. (See appendix for breakdown.)

 02 Budgets for other aspects of the work have not materially changed. Costs for workflow, API linking, and operational aspects remain steady.

 03 Work required for reports identified since June last year has not been factored in.

Title of each page is the message

This means we need to make trade-offs when rescoping the project workplans

Option 1

Spend $1.2m more now or $2m more later

We could deliver
- everything in FY23 with $1.2m more during FY23
- some in FY23, some in FY24 with $2m or more in total.

Option 2

Renegotiate scope or time with the regulator

We could
- limit the scope to delivering only the top 70 reports by FY23 within the current budget and negotiate with the regulator to accept this as final
- seek agreement from the regulator to further extend project timelines.

Repetitive wording removed and language tightened

We ask you to advise which trade-offs we can make

We need to decide whether we

Spend more by
1. increasing funding by $1.2m for FY23
2. budgeting $2m more for the project in total and roll into next year.

Renegotiate by
1. accepting the top 70 reports in FY23 as adequate and convincing the regulator to agree
2. seeking extensions from the regulator.

Email templates

Pre-formatted email signatures

These are available for download in the Clarity Hub, or alternatively you can copy type them from here.

Email signature idea #1

Hello xxx ...

['WHAT': Introduce the topic you wish to discuss in a way that is relevant right now]

['WHY': Explain why you wish to discuss this topic in this email]

[MAIN MESSAGE – Articulate a single, powerful and overarching message in 25 words or less]

- [Support 1]
- [Support 2]
- [Support 3 – if needed]
- [Support 4 – if needed]
- [Support 5 – if needed]

I hope that helps.

Cheers,
Dav

Email signature idea #2

Hello xxx ...

Using a visual layout helps both you and your audience to see the hierarchy of your messaging. This template is here to remind you how to do that.

In short, use formatting to signal which part of the structure each element belongs to. In more detail:

- Make the main message pop off the page using white space and bold.
- Use bullets and/or numbers to encourage you to break out your points and avoid 'block shock'.
- Break up sections that are longer than three lines so your audience can find your point without working too hard.

I hope that helps.

Cheers,
Dav

Email to help your colleagues understand your approach

I have included a copy of this in the Clarity Hub Toolkit. Equally, you could copy it from here.

Hi colleague/boss,

I have been thinking about *X* issue and have outlined my early thinking on a page for your consideration.

Before you review it, I'd like to explain how the page works so the diagram makes sense to you.

1. **It is a discussion draft.** Although the ideas are I hope in a clear and logical place within the structure, the ideas are very much open for debate.

2. **The draft outlines my current thinking in a way that may seem more direct than usual.** You will see that the ideas are anchored around a single message that is crafted as a point of view. The technique I am using flushes out the main thought up-front, before diving into the details.

3. **Once we agree on the messaging, we can turn these ideas into a well-structured document.** I would like to hold off on preparing the document until we agree on the ideas to minimise rework. Focusing on the one-pager first will keep us focused on the main ideas and encourage us to 'nail these' without being distracted by document formatting. My experience so far suggests we can save time this way.

I look forward to discussing issue *X* with you further in our upcoming meeting.

Regards,

Fred

Appendix

▲ Leaders' toolkit

Clarity Club Plan

Week 0 **Get started**	Week 1 **Clarify outcome**	Week 2 **Use patterns**	Week 3 **Firm up messaging**	Week 4 **Settle documents**
0	**01**	**02**	**03**	**04**

Week 0	Week 1	Week 2	Week 3	Week 4
> Explain why you are doing this > Confirm logistics, allowing about an hour each week for individual learning and time to practice on live work. > Provide PowerPoint Planner to all > Set homework – Ask them to read the introduction plus chapters 1, 2 & 3 of the *Engage* book or complete all Foundation & Strategy modules from the *Engage* course	**Reflect –** > Message mapping process > Stakeholder needs > Desired outcome **Ask –** > Where have you understood stakeholders well? Where have you not? > Where could you use the ideas next? > Insights so far? **Challenge –** > Map key stakeholders for current communication **Extend –** > Read Chapter 4 of *Engage* or complete the Frame Your Messaging modules from the online course > Practise with first email every day	**Reflect –** > Patterns as useful short cut **Ask –** > Where have you tried a pattern? Which one? > Which ones might become your 'go to'? **Challenge –** > Pick a pattern and use it to draft an email > Use a pattern to sketch out a message map together **Extend –** > Read Chapter 5 of *Engage* or complete the Firm Up Your Messaging modules from the online course. > Build and peer review a message map for a live communication	**Reflect –** > First principles help squeeze out the insights **Ask –** > Have you used SCORE yet? > Have you collaborated to build a message map? > Can you share an example? **Challenge –** > Scan and SCORE a one-page message map > Scan and SCORE an email first and then a more complex doc **Extend –** > Complete remaining chapters or modules from *Engage* > Require message maps for all future papers	**Reflect –** > Your observations of changes in emails and other docs **Ask –** > Have you completed a whole map to doc cycle? > What templates do we need to adjust? **Challenge –** > Review the prose and PowerPoint examples **Extend –** > Decide how to handle templates so they align with message mapping principles > See chapter 9 in *Elevate* for ideas for you and your champions to embed the approach into the longer term

Workshop Schedule

LEARN	DO	PURPOSE	ACTIVITY	TIMER
10		Familiarise all with the plan	Welcome and introduce the session	0
10		Focus everyone on approach	Before and after exercise	10
5	15	Develop communication strategy	Appreciate that you must take time to think through your engagement strategy before drafting your message	20
5	15	Structure the introduction	Clarify the question they want to set the audience up to ask	40
5	5	Synthesise main message	Articulate the main message in a sentence	1 hr
15		Structure supporting ideas	Familiarise with both grouping and deductive structures, focus on groupings	1 hr 10
	10	**BIO BREAK**		**1 hr 20**
	30	Build out supporting structure for message map, iterate to improve	Apply the ideas, consolidating by building a real example	1 hr 50
5	15	Review message map using SCORE framework	Consolidate concepts, reaffirm the value of collaborating to get to a better story sooner	2 hr 10
5		Learn to telegraph the hierarchy of the messaging	Close the conceptual loop between the message map and the document	2 hr 15
	15	Convert message map into a paper or presentation	Practice linking a message map to a real communication	2 hr 30
	15	Next steps and debrief	Make it stick!	2 hr 45

Workshop Kit details

If you're planning a workshop to train your team on the message map process but would prefer not to build your own exercises and examples, I offer a fully annotated workshop kit.

It offers the tools you need to run a practical program as well as videos to guide your way. This includes two key elements: the guided toolkit and resources to help with embedding the approach.

A guided toolkit for running a practical program

You can decide whether you or one of your champions delivers this workshop. It includes everything you need to facilitate a quick kick-off to set expectations and run the three-hour workshop, and more to support you in embedding the approach into your operating rhythm.

The Kit includes the following:

- ▲ PowerPoint slides to introduce concepts, exercises and reflections across three two-hour workshops
- ▲ a facilitator's guide, including frequently asked technical message mapping questions
- ▲ tools and templates for you and the team to use when putting message mapping into practice
- ▲ annotated templates for board papers
- ▲ ideas for adopting the structured thinking approach inside sometimes restrictive corporate templates.

Help with embedding the approach into your team's operating rhythm

Inside your Workshop Kit you will find supplementary tools such as exercises and videos. For example, my short email course is a great way to warm your team up before you dive into your program. I have cherry picked some case studies and exercises to help also. I also offer opportunities to connect with me directly.

Learn more at ClarityFirstProgram.com/WorkshopKit

(Please note: I will update this over time)

Pulse Check: key indicators

I suggest adding a pulse check into the agenda for the first team meeting of each month to thoroughly embed the habit. Use the following questions for this check:

What consistently occurs?

- Leaders discuss the desired outcome for key communication before teams draft anything?
- Substantive and potentially rigorous discussions about messaging are focused around one-page message maps before documents are drafted?
- Decisions are made quickly at leadership forums following rich discussions that involve minimal requests for clarification?

What rarely occurs?

- Leaders reworking team papers?
- Leadership forums rejecting papers that contain good ideas?
- 'Firefighting' stemming from poor communication?
- Lengthy, convoluted email chains?

References and further reading

Books

Aristotle (~4th century BC), *Rhetoric*

Bryar, C & Carr, B (2021), *Working Backwards*, St. Martin's Press

Drucker, P (2013), *People and Performance*, Harvard Business Review Press

Grant, A (2021), *Think Again*, Viking

Hyatt, M (2019), *Free to Focus*, Baker Publishing Group

Johnson, W (2022), *Smart Growth: How to Grow Your People to Grow Your Company*, Harvard Business Review Press

Kolko, J (2010), 'Abductive thinking and sensemaking: The drivers of design synthesis', *Design Issues*

Lombardo, M & Eichinger, R (2010), *The Career Architect Development Planner*, Lominger

McKeon, G (2021), *Effortless*, Currency

Medcalf, R (2022), *Making Time for Strategy*, Xquadrant

Minto, B (2021), *The Minto Pyramid Principle*, Pearson Education Limited

Minto, W (2018), *Logic, Inductive and Deductive*, Franklin Classics

Moore, MG (2021), *No Bullshit Leadership*, Rosetta Books

Newport, C (2016), *Deep Work*, Grand Central Publishing

Pink, D (2005), *A Whole New Mind*, Riverhead Books

Soojung-Kim Pang, A (2020), *Shorter*, Penguin General UK

Stanley, D & Castles, G (2017), *The So What Strategy*, Clarity Know How

Varol, O (2020), *Think like a Rocket Scientist*, WH Allen

Watson, D (2004), *Watson's Dictionary of Weasel Words*, Vintage Australia

Zelazny, G (2001), *Say it with Charts*, McGraw Hill

Zelazny, G (2006), *Say it with Presentations,* McGraw Hill

Tools and Downloads

Clarity Hub - ClarityFirstProgram.com/ClarityHub (first month free)

Email course - ClarityFirstProgram.com/Emails (free)

Printed in Australia
Ingram Content Group Australia Pty Ltd
AUHW012330230624
396082AU00002B/2

9 781923 007130